A NEW WINDMILL BOOK OF NON-FICTION

IT'S FOR REAL

EDITED BY ANGELA BARRS

Heinemann
New Windmills

Heinemann Educational Publishers
Halley Court, Jordan Hill, Oxford OX2 8EJ
A division of Reed Educational and Professional Publishing Ltd

OXFORD MELBOURNE AUCKLAND
JOHANNESBURG BLANTYRE GABORONE
IBADAN PORTSMOUTH (NH) USA CHICAGO

04 03 02 01 00
10 9 8 7 6 5 4 3 2 1

ISBN 0 435 130439

Acknowledgements
The Editor and Publishers would like to thank the following for permission to use
copyright material: The Anchor Trust for their leaflet 'Super-sleuths wanted!'; Random
House Group Ltd. for an extract from *When Daddy Came Home: How Family Life
Changed Forever in 1945,* by Barry Turner and Tony Rennell, published by
Hutchinson/Pimlico; The Rough Guides for an extract from *The Millennium: A Rough
Guide to the Year 2000,* 2nd edition 1999, by Nick Hanna; The Face Magazine for extracts
from the article '50 Revolutions per Minute'; Peters, Fraser & Dunlop Ltd. on behalf of
Blake Morrison for an extract from *And When Did You Last See Your Father?*, published
by Granta Books, 1998: Hodder and Stoughton Ltd. for extracts from *Behind the Smile,*
by Lisa Potts; Orion Publishing Group Ltd. for extracts from *Crazy Horse* by Larry
McMurty, published by Wiedenfeld and Nicholson, 1999; Robinson Publishing Ltd. for
extracts from *The Mammoth Book of War Diaries*, edited by Jon E. Lewis, 1998;
Independent Newspapers (UK) Ltd. for the article 'Teen sex? Play the waiting game for
best results', by Hester Lacey, in The Independent on Sunday, 26 July 1998; J17 Magazine
for the article 'Siblings for Sale!', by Sarah Gill, July 1998p Guardian Media Group plc for
two articles, 'Men are hopeless at talking . . .' by John Diamond and Nigella Lawson, in
The Observer, 17 May 1998, and 'Winners who lost everything', by Fergal Keane in The
Guardian, 9 January 1999; Select Magazine for the article 'In Residence', by Mark Morriss,
September 1998; The National Society for Clean Air and Environmental Protection for
extracts from their leaflet 'Neighbour Noise Problems'; The Controller of Her Majesty's
Stationery Office for extracts from the leaflet 'Air Pollution'; The Environment Agency for
extracts from their leaflet 'Floodline'; Treesponsibility for their leaflet 'Treesponsibility –
climate action in Calderdale'; Christian Aid for the advertisement 'This is your last chance
to support our team', produced for their Christian Aid Week Appeal, 1998; Professor
Audrey Osler for extracts from *Speaking Out: Black Girls in Britain*, published by Virago
Press, 1989; Oxfam GB for an extract and photographs from a mailing leaflet 'Oxfam's £2
a month', 1998, photographs by James Hawkins/Oxfam, Jenny Matthews/Oxfam and
Marian Pocock/Oxfam.

The Publishers have made every effort to trace the copyright holders, but if they have
inadvertently overlooked any, they will be pleased to make the necessary arrangements
at the first opportunity.

Cover by Rob Hefferan
Designed and produced by The Point
Typeset by Tek-Art, Croydon, Surrey
Printed and bound in the United Kingdom by Clays Ltd, St Ives plc

Contents

Introduction for Teachers

This book has been designed as a non-fiction reading resource with activities suitable for use with Key Stage 4 students across a range of abilities. The extracts and materials cover a variety of genres, from information leaflets, advertisements and flyers to biographical and journalistic writing. The range offers students a wide experience of non-fiction reading to help prepare them for GCSE terminal examinations.

Activities suggested at the end of each section include initial short tasks, leading to longer, more challenging ones with speaking and listening opportunities built in. Some of the tasks could be used for controlled practice to simulate exam conditions.

Above all, I hope readers will be stimulated by the issues presented in the texts. By responding to writers who speak to them about the real world, they can develop into perceptive and fluent communicators themselves.

Angela Barrs

Introduction for Students

The readings in this book offer you a variety of genres to explore. All of them are non-fiction texts covering aspects of people's lives in different times, situations and places. There are accounts of life written by children and pensioners, articles from magazines and newspapers, transcripts of interviews, accounts heard on the radio and suggestions for browsing the Internet. The readings are arranged in five sections, each with a thematic focus, to help you see similarities and differences between texts in each section.

In addition, the readings should help you to prepare for examinations at the end of Key Stage 4 in English. Your teacher may select some of the tasks from the end of each section to support you in this.

The real world speaks to you through these texts. I hope that you find a variety of readings to interest you.

Angela Barrs

Section 1
The Time of Our Lives

Moments which stick in our memories are those such as the first day at primary school or winning an important match or competition. As we mature, we realize that each decade produces changes not only in our personal situations but also for human beings generally. Some events assume greater or lesser importance: airships never did become a serious challenge to aeroplanes; leeches, used by medieval doctors and rejected as a quack's remedy, may yet prove valuable in hi-tech medicine. The writers in this section tell you what seemed important at a particular time. Some ask you to consider which events will have a lasting impact on future human development. As you read, you can compare your life experiences with those described and speculate on which 'big revolutions' in the way we live now will turn out to be lasting and which will become just bits of trivia. Will tomorrow's brilliant invention become nothing more than a footnote in a history textbook?

Extract 1: from 'Children and the War', *The Natural Development of the Child*, by Agatha Bowley (page 3)

These are several short wartime accounts, written by Scottish children in 1941 and 1942.

Extract 2: *Super-sleuths wanted!*, Anchor Trust (page 5)

The Anchor Trust is a charity which collects the true stories of older people in order to 'save a piece of history'. This leaflet asks people to submit their memories of life after the Second World War to prevent later generations forgetting recent history.

Extract 3: from *When Daddy Came Home: How Family Life Changed Forever in 1945*, by Barry Turner and Tony Rennell (page 8)

Wartime affected domestic life very much. When soldiers took home leave or returned to civilian life awkward adjustments were sometimes inevitable at home. Each child in this extract tries to work out how to respond to the newcomer in the home.

Extract 4: from *The Millennium: A Rough Guide to the Year 2000*, by Nick Hanna (page 13)

By the time you read this, we will be living in a new millennium. The months leading up to December 1999 were full of concerns about the 'millennium bug' and there were projects of all kinds to round off a thousand calendar years. Nick Hanna was one of the people reflecting on the lead up to, and the beginning of, the next one thousand years. This extract was published in 1998.

Extract 5: from '50 Revolutions per Minute', *The Face*, January 1997 (page 19)

The millennium has come and gone, along with endless predictions for the future, and reviews of what went before. Extract 5, from the January 1997 edition of *The Face* magazine, selects six out of fifty ideas from that decade which had some impact on the culture and environment. Some of these have grown in importance, others have sunk without trace.

Extract 1: *Children and the War*

David (9), Elma (10), Kenneth and James (both about 11) write about what they miss most in wartime:

DAVID I miss the lamps in the streets for I went out evry night. I do miss sweets that my mother got for me. I miss apple pie. I miss it for my mother could not get cooking apples aniwhere she been at many shops trien to get them. I miss getting out at night to play with outher boys I miss getting away my holyday to Arbroath where I went every year.

ELMA I am going to write about the things I miss most. The first thing is bananas. I used to get them nearly every morning to my breakfast with sugar and milk. They were delicious. Secondly I miss the great variety of sweets. You used to go into the shops and ask for any kind of sweets and get as much as you wanted.

Another thing I miss is the gaily coloured lights which used to light signs above shop doors. Well, I think I shall stop now as that is all the things I miss most.

KENNETH There is many things that I miss in war-time so I will wright them. I miss the sweets I got because I liked them. The next thing I miss is my father he is away to the Navy. My father has a shop but my mother works in it now that father is away. I take bad with seeing the white lines on the road. Off course the drivers of the motter cars need these to guide themselves in the blackout. I miss the lamp-posts and the lamp-

lighters at nights. Last year at Christmas I missed all the presents, and on my birthday I didn't get any presents because there is nothing to buy.

JAMES The things Imiss are chocolate and th butiful shop windows all lit up, and apples and oranges and all other different kinds of fruit likes of grapes and strawberries and tomatoes. And bananas. And to sit beside the river and watch all the steamers and all the yatchys heading for the

Extract 2: *Super-sleuths Wanted!*

1946	First calculator
1946	Launch of the NHS
1948	First full-size supermarket opens in London
1949	Flight of the world's first jet airliner
1949	First launderettes opened
1950	Eagle comic is launched
1951	Zebra crossings introduced
1952	First Top 10 chart appears in New Musical Express

Super-sleuths wanted!

Help Anchor Trust save a piece of history for older people by finding the stories of those who built the post-war world.

The 1995 VE day and VJ day celebrations did much to remember and record the experiences of those who fought or lived through the Second World War.

But less well known are some of the experiences and important achievements that took place in the post-war period of the late 1940s and 50s. It was then that many of the seeds were sown for the enormous technological and social changes that have shaped the way we now live. The stories of the generation that witnessed the birth of the post-war world should not be lost.

1952 First teabags appear in shops

1953 DNA discovered by Cambridge scientists

1955 Commercial television starts (1st TV ad was for SR toothpaste)

1956 £1 Premium Bonds introduced

1958 First parking meters come to London

1959 Hovercraft developed

1959 First charity walk

With your help Anchor would like to give older people a chance to tell those stories and save a piece of history.

To make this happen Anchor Trust is collecting first-hand accounts of the period, which we aim to publish in a book marking the end of the millennium. We are therefore asking older people and their relatives and friends to find and send us these accounts.

Do you know someone who was involved in something new and innovative during this period (e.g. worked on the first jet engines in 1949 or the first motorway in 1958)? Do you know someone whose life was affected by the great changes taking place (e.g. moved to one of the 'new towns' built in 1946 or worked in commercial television, which began in 1955)?

If so, we'd like to hear from you. Your story might make history.

Anchor Trust is the leading charity providing care and housing for older people in England.

Extract 3: *When Daddy Came Home*

Sandy Gardner

My earliest clear memory is of berating some council workmen who were taking a tea-break from some clearing-up in our back green.

'C'mon youse,' I said. 'Mah Daddy's comin' hame fae the war next week and Ah want this place lookin' nice for him.'

The first thing that was special about the Big Day was that I got to ride in a car for the first time – an unheard-of luxury in those days! There was no way that our returning hero was going to travel the final leg of this journey home on a bus or train – so my grandpa hired a taxi to take me and my mum the 20-mile round trip into Glasgow to meet my dad.

Queen Street Station was packed with people. I have a very clear picture of the engine of the troop train when it arrived. It was steam-driven, of course, and had an enclosed boiler. The engine and carriages were very dirty on the outside. As the train drew into the station, the driver gave a long blast on his hooter and everyone – the soldiers in the train and the families on the platform – all started cheering.

Me – I nearly jumped out of my skin. And then he was there.

We were soon back in the taxi being driven home to Bellshill in great style. As soon as we arrived I went out the back – the common space around which the tenement flats were grouped – and rounded up all of the children I could find. They were then ushered into my grandma's kitchen, where my dad was sitting by the fire – still wearing his uniform.

When all my pals were duly assembled, I pointed at my father and announced as loudly as I could – 'That's mah Daddy!'

Most of the other kids' fathers worked in the steelworks and had not been called up for military service. I was one of the few who had grown up without a father in the house. Now I had a dad just like them –

And I was awful proud of him.

Muriel Woodhead

My twin sister and I looked forward to our father's return from India where he had served as a captain. As the day approached I was filled with a sickening dread, I remember sitting on my bed and praying the **incongruous** prayer, 'O God, if there is a God, let me recognize my father.' The fear of not recognizing him and worse still, knowing that I had not recognized him dominated my waking moments. The scene remains vivid. Above all I remember the hot embarrassment and shame. Surely no good child could fail to recognize her own father? He would cross the threshold and be a stranger and my non-recognition would reveal the unpardonable sin – I didn't love my father.

This sense of my father being a stranger persisted through the rest of my childhood and adolescence. After he died and I heard people

---

incongruous out of place; used here in the sense 'illogical' talking about him, I realized that I had never really known him. The long absence during the war and the strains the war had put on those left behind took such a toll that the threads of a happy family relationship were never fully recovered. I am sure it was so for others.

The most cheerful recollections are of the exotic presents and souvenirs he brought back from India – the perfumed wonder of real Turkish delight, a whole glutinous box full, lengths of sari silk, and leather-thonged sandals and satchels embossed with elephants and smelling mysteriously of dusty bazaars and ships' holds. The contrast with the grim realities of wartime austerity was exquisitely potent.

But such pleasures faded as he became ill. A rash covered his skin, the result we were told of some tropical disease. We were 'shushed' if we made a noise and crept around on tiptoe. The doctor came and went. The house was filled with antiseptic smells and steaming bowls of potassium permanganate were carried to his room. When he did appear his skin was dyed indigo. Looking back I wonder if the rash was in part **psychosomatic**, caused by the stress of trying to adjust to family life.

So much was hoped for. Just old enough to remember the pre-war days, Muriel was desperate to recover the secure routines of the old life. But there could be no putting the clock back.

---

psychosomatic brought on by the mind

The most bizarre attempt my parents made to recover 'normality' was to spend most of my father's demobilization gratuity on a holiday. That would be the **panacea**, it was felt, for all emotional and physical ills and would bring us together again as a family. It was a disaster. A trip to London coincided with an electric storm of such alarming ferocity as to leave me numb with fear. The crashing of thunder directly overhead and bolts of lightning hitting rooftops nearby was so reminiscent of the bombing that I lost my power of speech for a while and became **catatonic** with shock. This was followed by a wretched fortnight in Yorkshire. It rained the entire time. Ghastly boarding houses and awful landladies quibbling over rations. We returned sick and exhausted with the money gone and nothing to show for it. The fragile relationships within the family could not withstand even trivial anxieties like the non-arrival of a train, which meant waiting for hours without food on a cold platform. The 'bonding' which was meant to occur, the coming together of one happy family on holiday, with Daddy safely back in charge, did not happen. Nor could it ever happen.

Muriel adds:
We honour our war dead. But there were other 'deaths' which have not been written about or

panacea healing medicine
catatonic in a stupor; unresponsive state

commemorated. Recollections of victory are often rose-coloured, high with the excitement of street parties and bunting and ribbons of welcome for returning heroes. But for some families the experience was far more complex than that.

Extract 4: *The Millennium: A Rough Guide to the Year 2000*

Why is there so much interest in the year 2000?

Ever since humanity became conscious of the fact just over a few hundred years ago that it was living 'in' a particular decade or century, people have tended to define their era by reference to groups of ten or a hundred years. We review a decade in terms of society's achievements and failures, natural disasters and other events, while at the same time looking forward to what might be on the horizon in the decade ahead. A century-long span offers an additional **nuance**, since it is at the upper limits of human life expectancy.

It is hardly surprising, therefore, that the year 2000 should carry with it some conceptual force, not to mention the weight of religious and millennial expectations. The magnetic pull it exerts is partly explained by the fact that it is the first time in history that so many people have shared the consciousness that a thousand-year time cycle is about to come to a close.

Even though cynics maintain that it is no more than a roll-over of digits on the clock, and party-poopers claim that the millennium doesn't start until 2001, the year 2000 has already generated a huge volume of features in the media, dozens of books on everything from millennial prophecies to the millennium time bomb, and hundreds of Web sites.

'The millennium is the comet that crosses the calendar every thousand years. It throws off metaphysical sparks. It promises a new age, or an apocalypse. It is a magic trick that time performs, extracting a millisecond from its eternal flatness and then, poised on that transitional instant, projecting a sort of hologram that teems with the summarized life of a thousand years just passed and with visions of the thousand now to come.'
Time, Fall 1992

---

nuance shade, degree (of interest)

What is the millennium time bomb?

Also known as the Y2K (Year 2000) problem, or simply the millennium bomb, it refers to the fact that computers all over the world may crash as their data systems roll 1999 over into 2000.

The problem originates with the design of early computer programmes, when memory was at such a premium that programmers shortened commands to a minimum whenever they could. This included shortening the year to just two numbers (ie '56' instead of 1956) so that the date came to be represented as DD/MM/YY (08/03/56, for example). Although this seems like a tiny saving, dates occur so often in software systems that it saved memory space many times over, and programmers had no idea that these original computer languages would still be operating at the end of the century.

With the development of more powerful computers, the logic for this abbreviation has long since disappeared, but meanwhile it had become standard convention throughout the programming world.

As 1999 clicks over into 2000 the computer will register only '00', recognizing the year as 1900 rather than 2000. It may then become confused, believe it has been tampered with, and shut down altogether. British tourists to the US have been aware of this **anomaly** for over a decade, since their driving licences, which have expiry dates well into the next century, were being rejected by the computer systems of car rental companies.

Experts warn of disruption on a worldwide scale, as everything from cash dispensers to air traffic control systems and elevators begins to malfunction. Almost everything containing a microchip could be at risk. Some people predict that as dawn breaks over the Pacific and spreads across the globe, up to 50,000 mainframes will crash in succession, causing a wave of economic, political and social chaos that will engulf the entire world.

The nightmare scenario could well result in a situation

anomaly out of the ordinary, deviation from the rule

where databases that normally calculate taxes, pensions, mortgages and utility bills suddenly begin to churn out rubbish. Children might be sent pensions and pensioners might automatically be added to primary school intake lists; a hundred years of interest could be added to savings accounts, or vice versa, with massive amounts in interest debited to credit cards or bank balances. Everything from military hardware to civilian aircraft may be simultaneously scheduled for maintenance.

On the home front, 'slave' chips that control domestic appliances could go similarly awry. You might wake up with a hangover on January 1, 2000 to find the burglar alarm going off, the refrigerator defrosting, the boiler shut down, and the video and microwave simply failing to function. Don't think you can escape chaos by leaping in your car and driving away. If it has a chip controlling its engine, it won't start. You won't be able to catch the train either, since computers that control key safety systems such as signalling and power supplies would have shut down.

Things that might go haywire on January 1, 2000

Aeroplanes, air conditioners, air traffic control systems, automatic doors, bar code readers, cafeteria equipment, cameras, cars, cash registers, clocks, credit card scanners, electronic vaults, emergency lighting, escalators, fax machines, fire alarms, fridge/freezers, heating systems, helicopters, hospital equipment, lifts, lighting systems, medical equipment, microwaves, military hardware, missile systems, motorized wheelchairs, optical readers, pagers, photocopiers, postage meters, power management systems, printers, satellite receivers, scanners, security gates, telephones, thermostats, time clocks, traffic lights, vending machines, video recorders, water heaters.

Every single computer in existence has an embedded clock, and most software features a mathematical representation of the date. On January 1, 2000, the two-digit format ceases to function. This is what amounts to the millennium time bomb.

It has already been called the biggest human-made disaster to hit the information technology industry. It is, in fact, a wonderfully appropriate and ironic apocalyptic scenario for millennial expectations in the age of the computer.

Nostradamus

Born in Provence in 1503, Michel de Nostradame is the most famous prophet of the last thousand years, and his predictions have been studied avidly for the last four and a half centuries. He was known simply as Nostradamus (the Latinized version of his name), and his predictive talents were encouraged by his grandfather, who was physician to King René of Provence. Having shown an early aptitude for astrology and maths, Nostradamus was sent to study the arts in Avignon, but upset his teachers by defending astrology and the theories of Copernicus. He then studied medicine at Montpellier and became well known as a plague doctor before losing his own wife and children to the Black Death when he was just 34.

Nostradamus wandered in self-imposed exile in Italy and southern Europe, the tragedy turning his energies inwards to the occult for the next ten years, a time during which he is said to have developed his prophetic vision. In 1544 he returned to Provence, married a rich widow and devoted himself whole-heartedly to the predictive arts. He began writing an annual almanac and was sufficiently encouraged by its success to embark on what was to become his most famous work, the seven-volume *Centuries*, intended as a future history of the world.

In 1556 Nostradamus predicted the death of Henry II of France in a jousting accident, which drew him to the attention of the queen, Catherine de Medici. In 1559 Henry II was duly killed as foreseen, making Nostradamus the talk of the courts of Europe. Crowds burned effigies of him before the Inquisitors, and he was only rescued from death by Catherine, who later encouraged Charles IX to elevate him to the status of Counsellor and Physician in Ordinary.

Just eighteen months later, Nostradamus died as he himself had prophesied: 'On his return from the embassy, the King's gift put in place. He will do nothing more. He will be gone to God. Close relatives, friends, brothers by blood will find him completely dead near the bed and the bench.'

Nostradamus's *Centuries* comprises a series of 942 four-line quatrains. Written in a combination of French, Latin, Greek and Provençal, the poetic and obscure nature of the prophecies has proved a fruitful source of material for interpreters, who have been able to read into them whatever they want. Nostradamus consciously made them **enigmatic**, jumbling time sequences and historical **allusions** to protect himself against potential repercussions.

Century 3, Quatrain 95

This particular quatrain is said by commentators, among them Stefan Paulus, to have predicted the fall of communism:

The Law of More people
will be seen to fall:
After a different one a
good deal more seductive:
Dnieper first will fall:
Through gifts and language to
another more attractive.

'More' as used here is said to refer to Sir Thomas More, who published his *Utopia* when Nostradamus was a student, the inference being that utopia was an allegory for communism. Democracy is seen as a 'different one' (political system) which replaced communism because it was 'a good deal more seductive'. The Dnieper runs through Kiev, the capital of the Ukraine, which was one of the first breakaway states from the USSR. And the transition came about peacefully, 'through gifts' (pledges of aid) and 'language' (diplomacy).

enigmatic with a hidden meaning
allusions references

Century 10, Quatrain 72

Dozens of volumes have been written on Nostradamus's enigmatic quatrains, all of them offering different interpretations, but most scholars seem to agree that the prophet's most compelling prediction concerning the millennium is Century 10, Quatrain 72:

The year 1999,
* the seventh month,*
From the sky will come
* a great King of Terror;*
Resuscitating the great
* King of the Mongols,*
Before and after Mars
* to reign happily.*

It is one of the very few quatrains to mention a specific date but, despite this, some argue that the original French word 'sept' might be short for September. The 'great King of Terror' is thought to imply the imminent arrival of a comet, which would collide with the planet, or indeed a nuclear war. The reference to the King of the Mongols, Genghis Khan, is interpreted as pointing the finger at north-west China, but there again, others maintain that the reference alludes to an advanced alien civilization which will be able to clone Genghis Khan's cells to resurrect the Antichrist. Some commentators have also made much of the proximity of this date to a major planetary alignment which will take place in August 1999, when the last solar eclipse of the century will be followed by a Grand Cross of the planets in the fixed signs of the zodiac (Taurus, Leo, Scorpio and Aquarius) which correspond to the Four Horsemen of the Apocalypse in John's Revelation.

The only prediction that is 100 per cent certain is that books on Nostradamus will continue to be churned out well into the next millennium.

Extract 5: *50 Revolutions per Minute*

DIRECT ACTION

Society is changing faster than the main political parties can, forcing them to abandon ideology for short-term vote-chasing; and with neither Blair nor Major offering programmes for change, many voters have chosen to take direct action over single causes. Much has been made of odd alliances between middle-class Middle Englanders and New Primitivists at demos; in truth the latter are likely to be the former's offspring.

THE INTERNET

After years during which the Internet sounded like some addled cyberpunk fantasy (remember cyberpunks?), it's now hard to imagine a world without those http://www addresses that lend a spurious techno-sheen to so many print and TV ads. Those with the hardware to connect to those World Wide Web addresses – the information 'haves' – now take for granted a transglobal glut of graphically-enhanced amusement and information. Roll on flat-rate local calls from BT, so that the UK can start bingeing on the Internet like the rest of the world.

INFANTILISM

Infantilization has gone well beyond early-Nineties kiddie fashions like baby-doll dresses and ravers' dummies to become a more long-term condition. Adults collecting Star Wars toys; adverts referring to 'Seventies kids' TV; trash food from childhood is revisited ironically. Growing up has never been such (childish) fun.

SUPERDISEASES

Just as the medical community puts its full intellectual weight behind Aids research, we get the return of the golden oldies. TB was the first to rear its ugly Victorian

---

spurious false

head again, but the re-emergence of cholera and diphtheria sparked the World Health Organization to announce the birth of 'superviruses': common diseases that have developed new antibiotic-resistant strains. And if those don't get you, there's always Ebola, Hepatitis C, BSE and CJD and, by no means least, Streptococcus, the 'necrotizing fasciitis' (that's 'flesh-eating bacteria from hell' to you, matey).

RAGE-ISM

Road rage, cinema rage, trolley rage . . . impatience, frustration and uncontainable anger – at anything from social injustice to bad art to a traffic jam – has caused random and seemingly mindless violence to be visited upon the next poor sod down the line. Some argue that this increasingly common inability to exercise self-control is a direct consequence of The Moral Crisis. Sporadic, unpredictable and sometimes fatal, it has created a new victim culture. And it's not only the victim of the rager's spleen who is to be pitied: according to the assailants they, too, are the innocent victims of circumstance.

THE MORAL CRISIS

It's fitting that one of the most dysfunctional family units in Nineties Britain is the Windsors. Blind loyalty from their subjects has been eroded by cynicism and scandal. And if the Head of the Church of England can't instil the sanctity of marriage in her own children, what hope is there for the rest of us? Corrupt MPs in sex scandals we could accept: but what's it come to when teachers refuse to work until someone gets rid of their pupils, when your local bobby is armed with CS gas, and our sports stars are self-confessed cheats and wife-beaters?

Activities

1   **a**   Read the four short accounts by David, Elma, Kenneth and James in Extract 1. Which things to eat did the children miss most?

     b   Several features in the language of this extract show that the writers are young children. Quote three examples of these and suggest how more mature writers might express those ideas. (Do not restrict your choice to examples of misspellings.)

     c   The four children comment on the appearance and atmosphere of their neighbourhood in wartime. Try to imagine their childhood environment and briefly compare it with your own neighbourhood to show similarities or differences.

2   Read Extracts 1 and 2. Imagine yourself interviewing either the group of children, now grown up, from Extract 1 or some of your own elderly relatives or neighbours. You want to hear about their childhoods. Make up your own list of interview questions, remembering to ask not only for facts, but also for their feelings and opinions about that time in their lives.

3   Read the two accounts in Extract 3.

     a   Write a paragraph about the way Sandy communicates with the council workers and her friends. Comment on the style of her language, and on what it reveals about her attitude to her father, the council workers and her friends.

b Write a short note as if you were Muriel's father
ill in bed on his return home. Explain to your
daughter what has happened and how you
hope things will get better for the whole family.

4 Reflect on the information in Extract 4, which
was published in 1998. You are reading this *after*
the turn of the century. Write an article for your
school magazine, using the title: *Were they right
to worry?* Consider the concerns that people had
pre-millennium and whether they have, in your
opinion, been justified or not. Your readers are
people like yourself: select appropriate language
and state your views in a way which they will enjoy
reading in your school magazine. Try visiting one or
more websites to research this topic, for example:

http://www.millennium.gov.uk (the main
    government website) or
http://www.ast.cam.ac.uk (Royal Greenwich
    Observatory) or
http://www.skywebs.com/earthportals/
    milenport.html (Millennium Portal)

for ideas on what the twenty-first century holds.
You might search the web listings for 'millennium',
'apocalypse' or 'doomsday' for other ideas.

5 Read Extract 5. Rank the six 'revolutions' according
to which you think have made the greatest (top
place) and which the least impact on your world.
Argue your case for the positions you chose.
Alternatively, choose your own six revolutions of the
last ten years, and argue your case for these.

6 Read through all the extracts in Section 1. They all
deal with important events. What events would *you*
consider 'important'? Select two events to describe –

in the past, in the present or still to come. One should have a personal importance for you and another should have a wide significance for the human race. Describe each happening as vividly as you can, using imagination as well as research if necessary. Explain clearly why you consider each event to be 'important'.

Section 2
Transforming Influences

People, places and incidents influence us as we go through life. Some influences are so powerful that they affect us and change the way we are. Often the changes are sad, but some of them are uplifting. Others are so subtle and routine that we may not recognize their effect on us. This section looks at events or experiences that have had a lasting influence on people's lives.

Extract 1: from *And When Did You Last See Your Father?* by Blake Morrison (page 27)

In this memoir, Blake Morrison writes about the day after his father died. His relationship with his father, a local doctor, had been marked with difficulties and sadness. Although he is greatly affected by his father's death, the extract also shows his awareness of life continuing around him.

Extract 2: *Heard on the Radio* (page 34)

Last year, I turned the radio on whilst preparing a meal for friends and listened to people talking about their experiences of food in institutions. I felt particularly lucky to be in my own kitchen, cooking food I had chosen. I was looking forward to hearing the latest news from close friends that evening. The people whose tales I heard were not so fortunate: they sometimes missed out on the whole food experience. Adults and children talked about their food experiences in schools, children's homes and prisons. You can almost hear the speakers in this extract. Perhaps they are voicing some of your own feelings about food.

Extract 3: from 'The Lisa Potts Story', *The Mirror*, 16 June 1998 (page 37)

This is from Lisa Potts' autobiography and recounts the day that she had to protect the children in her care from a violent attack. Her heroism meant 'her own life changed beyond compare' in the words of the newspaper which bought her story.

Extract 4: from *Crazy Horse*, by Larry McMurtry (page 42)

In South Dakota, a family of sculptors is carving a horse and rider out of the mountain. It will take several generations to expose the whole statue in the rock. When they do so, the arm of Crazy Horse, the subject of this extract, will stretch almost the length of a football pitch. Much has been written about the US–Indian wars of 1865 to 1890, yet there is very little factual evidence about Crazy Horse, the legendary Sioux warrior.

He was not actually a chief of the Sioux or of any Indian clan, yet as a warrior, he was widely known and respected for his bravery and honesty not only by Indians of the Great Plains, but by the US army too. Soldiers like Crook tried to persuade the nomadic Indian tribes to settle in 'protected' reserves. This way, the wagon trains could roll westward across the plains safely. The Battle of the Little Bighorn became a legendary showdown, yet no one knows precisely *how* Crazy Horse fought in it. We *do* know that after he agreed to become an agency Indian,* he lost the trust of both sides. Perhaps that was why he

---

* A US government-paid Indian representing those settled in reserves or agencies. The army believed that if they could show Crazy Horse to be on their side, then more Indians would follow his example and Indian territory could be easily taken over.

never went to meet the US President in Washington to sign over Indian lands.

As the massive statue of Crazy Horse emerges from the rock in South Dakota, the myth growing around him has less and less to do with an ordinary man. This extract reflects first on the famous Battle of the Little Bighorn (June 25 and 26, 1876) and then on how Crazy Horse finally gave himself up to the whites, which inevitably resulted in his death.

Extract 5: from *The Mammoth Book of War Diaries and Letters*, edited by Jon E. Lewis (page 46)

Captain Albert Barnitz of the 7th Cavalry was also involved in the US–Indian wars and rode out against the Plains Indians during the 1868 expedition. Two years later at the Battle of Wounded Knee, the Great Plains were finally conquered and the Indians subdued. The last extract in this section comes from two of his letters home to his wife Jennie.

Extract 1: *And When Did You Last See Your Father?*

Three visits

The first day of life after his death. I walk to the café on Skipton High Street where we used to come after hours, boys from the grammar school, girls from the high school, cigarettes, a jukebox, coffee. This morning, school holidays and recession, I have the place nearly to myself. My appointment at the registry office isn't till twelve.

A girl comes in, blonde, eighteenish, white see-through blouse and flowery leggings under a long coat, pushing Maclaren buggy with a child of two inside, immaculately turned out. Shorter, younger, trim-jacketed, a boyfriend skulks behind. The girl is in charge: she slides a tray along the counter, loads it with cakes and drinks, pays at the till and turns, carrying the tray in one hand while pushing the buggy with the other. She chooses a table, parks the pushchair next to it and sits down on the green plastic bench, sliding her legs under the imitation marble tabletop. Some seconds after, as if reluctantly acknowledging he is of the same party, the boy takes the seat opposite, smug-looking, not saying a word to her, not looking at the baby either, who is churring happily with a bottle of thinned Ribena.

Is she a nanny or childminder? No, the baby calls her 'Mummy'. Is he the father? Hard to say. He doesn't seem to be a husband – neither of them wears a ring – but is he a partner? His lack of attention to both the girl and the baby is no kind of clue – it could just be shyness, or the domestic boredom of coupledom, or a northern male's assumption that pouring tea and petting babies falls outside his domain. But I can't get over how pleased with himself he looks. What's his power over the girl, that she sits there doing everything – leaning over now to wipe the face of her baby daughter, who's beginning to be restless in her pushchair straps, who's saying 'Mummy' pleadingly and wants to be out? The more the child whinges, the less a father he looks, the more that sullen-smug face of his suggests a different story: Look at me, I'm just seventeen and have an older woman who gives me her body, no trouble or lip or bills to pay. But if so, what's in it for her, what does she get from him? Her control, her copingness, seem to say: I can do better than this. But she's second fiddle to some smug, sullen, misogynistic berk.

The café has filled up a bit. I turn back to my paper, sneaking looks as the mother plays a slap-game with her daughter, a rhyming pat-a-cake routine which ends with her smacking the child's hands more vigorously than the game requires, harder than seems right. She turns to her consort, a bulge and swing in her blouse as she does so – unlike me, he looks away. Her face in profile is not a happy face, the top lip protrudes, the chin is rattily set back, more smoky anger in her than first seemed. Now the child, twenty minutes in captivity, is straining at its harness, whining, 'Lap, lap,' and the girl, tensing, worried they're becoming a spectacle, says loudly, loud enough to make people look across: 'Shut up. Wait till we're on the bus.' There's quiet for a bit, but then the child whines again, 'Mummy, lap,' not seeing what there is to wait for or why, and the whine turns into a cry, and now the girl leans over and slaps the child hard across the thighs. The child screams, less in pain than outrage, long shock-breaths between each cry. The mother and her lover sit silent and impassive, while the crying goes on under its own steam, nothing to do with them. An undeserved slap, a mother at the end of her nerves: no more than this, but there's a knot of awkwardness now, everyone in the café pretending not to have noticed but conversation faltering and silence gathering as reproach. I think of my father, soppy-stern most of the time (once, after I'd been cruel to my sister, he drew his fist back to hit me in the face but wasn't able to go through with it), occasionally a mad disciplinarian (his insistence I empty my plate, the smack I got for peeing in some bushes, the day he locked me in the cellar).What was kind and right, where did cruelty and neglect begin, what could you do that didn't damage your own life or your child's or both?

At last the girl stands up and begins to tidy cups, cutlery and napkins on to her tray. The boy, smug and wordless still, goes ahead of her to the door. The girl puts the tray down and unbrakes the pushchair – the child ceasing to cry now, aware something is happening – and out they go into the street, among other pushchairs, other people, the mill of bodies, the unending cycle of sex and parenthood, never enough time, never enough patience.

Anita M. Barnard wears a polite smile and an elegant grey dress. She likes to give a personal service, handwritten, no computerization. Friendly but not nosy, she holds a fountain pen and asks me to sit down. She needs to know, for the purposes of the form, who, when, where and how: she needs to know whether I was present at the time. But she does not want to talk about the death more than is strictly necessary, and if she ever knew my father (probably didn't – works six miles away, is under forty), she isn't letting on.

I give her his full name. The doctor's certificate says: Cause of death – Carcinoma 1(a).

'What does 1(a) mean?' I ask.

'Oh, that's a doctor's thing,' she explains. 'It means leading directly to death rather than a contributory factor, which is 1(b). When did he die?'

'Yesterday.'

She scritches away. 'Relation to the deceased?'

'Son.' I look at the map of Craven District on the wall, her patch of births, marriages and deaths. 'Are people fairly well in control of themselves by the time they come here?' I ask.

'Yes, usually, though you get some who want to talk about it and cry. Sometimes I want to cry myself in the really tragic cases – you know, like children.'

'But you don't just do deaths?'

'No, but this time of year, mostly. Today I've had four deaths, a birth and a marriage. Getting wed on a Monday morning – seems a bit odd to me, when they didn't have to, either. I'll just copy this out neatly and then we're done.'

I take the green cremation slip, the form for the DSS, the information booklets for widows, the death certificate itself. Outside on the notice-boards are the banns of intending couples. Four older men, MARR DISS, marrying younger women, SINGLE. A couple whose address is a barge on the Leeds–Liverpool canal. A twenty-two-year-old man marrying a thirty-eight-year-old woman. Not one old-fashioned marriage – people in their mid-twenties doing it for the first time. But then it's not the marrying season, not Whit or the hot blood of July. And my parent's wedding hadn't been so Mills and Boon either, by the look of the photos: registry office, half a dozen friends and relations huddled autumnally by a red brick wall, the war barely a year behind.

I shop for the wake at Morrisons, the big new supermarket where the old cattle mart used to be. My father had talked warmly of the place ('You can get any bloody thing you want') and bought shares in it, as if it were the family firm. I load the trolley high with drink – gin, whisky, brandy, vodka, rum, wine, lager, bitter, as much as I can get in, the booze mound, commemoration and amnesia. I have to hold the wine boxes at the top to prevent them falling out. A man in the queue behind me winks. The woman on the till gives a knowing smile: 'Now here's someone who's going to have a good Christmas.'

*

I drive to Airedale Hospital. Just along the corridor from Ward 19 is the postgraduate medical school, and in the library, among the BMJs and ghoulish textbooks, I see a woman, greying, fortyish, curatorial, who may be able to help. I explain: 'My father was a GP locally for thirty-five years. When he retired he donated some equipment here. He said that they were setting up a museum. I wonder if I could look. I wanted to see his donations.'

The woman seems a bit put out: this isn't routine. 'Sorry, it doesn't mean anything to me, I'm afraid. There's no actual museum, you see. We wanted one but we haven't the resources.'

'Not even an archive or display case or something?'

'We thought it would be good to have exhibits in the main reception, but it's against fire regulations: the law says you need acres of free floorspace. What's your father's name?'

'Dr Morrison. From Earby. He retired in 1976.'

'Well I've been here twenty years and I don't remember any bequest. But we do have a storeroom where various bits and pieces are kept.'

The storeroom is taken up with old medical journals, surplus from the library. On a high shelf are some little wooden boxes, beautifully made, chestnut-gleaming, with stethoscopes and other equipment under their sliding lids. It's cold in here but the woman is slowly warming to her task.

'We did have a few doctor's bags, with bottles in – the coloured sort, with stoppers. But thieves broke in – looking for drugs, the police thought – and they whipped them: they're the sort of thing you can sell at car boot sales. There's only this one left now.'

It's leather, and old, and grey – but it's not my father's.

'That's about it, I'm afraid, except for George.' She opens the lid of a large rough wooden box and pulls out a thighbone. She seems to relax, as if she's forgotten my being here is an irregularity and imposition, as if she's finally interested.

'We laid him out on the steps, a doctor and me, to see if he was all there. Of course they're made of plastic these days, the modern sort, not the real thing like George here.'

She takes out another off-white branch – a rib or arm.

'People feel funny about skeletons,' she says, 'but it never bothers me, coming in here, or working next door after dark knowing he's in his box. I rather like him.'

She stows the bones back in the box, shuts the lid and locks the door behind us. I thank her for her time. I'd hoped his old medical equipment might restore some part of my father to me, but thieves in the night had got there first.

In the car I wonder: had she been right about George being George? How different are male and female skeletons? Couldn't George have been Janet?

Extract 2: *Heard on the Radio*

Three men discussing their memories of school food remembered a dark-haired cook vividly, not for the food she prepared but for her black hairs in it. Finding one was like being cursed. As boys, they created other horror stories about food, such as the weekly dish they named 'resurrection pudding' because it re-used leftovers. 'Toenail pudding', with toenail-shaped caraway seeds, took its name from the chiropodist's Thursday visits. The men recalled hiding gristle or wormy potatoes under other bits of food, to avoid being ordered to finish their platefuls.

Dickens showed us similar scenes in *Nicholas Nickleby* where unlucky schoolboys were sent by rich parents to live on gruel at Dotheboys' Hall. We associate debtors' jails, orphanages and old folks' homes with miserable, cabbage-smelling, bleak fare. Food matters to us as much in schools and prisons as it does in any home. In one busy residential home, children and cooks talked together about food. Unlike the Dickensian regime, in West Yorkshire today children helped choose their menus, shopped and cooked meals. They listed pancakes, buns, muffins and omelettes amongst the dishes they cooked, including vegetarian meals. Their cook's list included home-made pizza, salad, baked potatoes and garlic bread and she insisted on young volunteers observing strict kitchen hygiene. In her kitchen, everyone knew about handwashing, wearing aprons and making sure that food such as fresh meat could not contaminate other food. But another young women who had left a residential home six years earlier said that her memories were not so positive. She remembered kitchens which were industrial, rather than welcoming and homely. Because the kitchens in homes she had lived in contained large fat-fryers, the children were prevented by health and safety regulations from using *any* of the utensils. Nutritionists and those working in children's charities know that being involved in budgeting, buying and preparing food is important for youngsters in care. These specialists believe children need to practise skills before leaving care in order to look after themselves independently from the age of sixteen. Not only do children need to do this as individuals, they also need to socialize with food, to cook and eat with other people. In old-style, residential homes where food was locked away and bought through bulk orders, there was little opportunity for children to participate in the food experience. Now, homes are smaller, with pleasant kitchens and the food is bought with cash in the supermarket. Using cash also gives practical experience of budgeting for real menus.

Adults don't always have similar opportunities. In prisons, food is not like home cooking. In prison, porridge *really* is served at breakfast. At mealtimes, many prisoners come together to collect their food and, if the quality or amount of food is inadequate, then they discuss their feelings about it. Mealtimes can become occasions for rioting. Inmates' restricted diet is supplemented with what they buy in the 'tuck shop'. They can spend the money earned in prison there. Some ethnic minority prisoners may save the meat from a meal and cook it in their cells with herbs and spices secretly brought in by visitors. Eating outside prison is usually a communal activity but prison cuts across that human need to connect with other people. It can lead to prisoners having strange food-based fantasies. One prisoner told a researcher how he lay in bed at night fantasizing about fried eggs, and imagined yolk running down over the toast. Inmates completing a long prison sentence often lose some of their social skills through lack of practice. They eat alone much of the time, in their cells or only with a cellmate. Adjusting to mealtimes as a communal activity is hard for them.

Research suggests that if you do live in an institution of some kind, then you eat institutionalized food. The food you eat is limited to what the institution provides and you may have little choice about it. That lack of control over what you eat, whether you are a child or an adult, can affect well-being. Physically and psychologically, food is very important to us and, if we have no control over it, there can be a high level of frustration.

Extract 3: *The Lisa Potts Story*

EXCLUSIVE: THE LISA POTTS STORY

I cried as I stepped on to the playground again . . it wasn't the place I'd loved

WHEN nursery nurse Lisa Potts saved the lives of a classroom of toddlers her own life changed beyond compare.

She received the George Medal for her courageous act of shielding the children against maniac Horrett Campbell as they held a teddy bears' picnic.

Here, in an extract from her book, *Behind the Smile*, she tells of her pain and anguish as she battles to come to terms with what happened at St Luke's Primary School in Wolverhampton.

Adapted by CLARE RAYMOND

'**AFTER four hours of surgery I regained consciousness at just after one o'clock in the morning.**

I had four severed tendons in my left hand – one had been cut twice – and there was a severed tendon in my right index finger.

I had had a plate put in my left arm where my ulna bone had been severely fractured.

My skull had been chipped and there were two lacerations on my back, one by the left shoulder and the other down the centre of my back, very close to my spine.

Yet when the ambulance men had arrived at the school they asked if I wanted a stretcher and I said: "No, I can walk."

I couldn't let the children see me being carried out – they would think I was dead. Nicola (the other nursery nurse) wanted to come to the hospital with me, but there was no room in the ambulance.

"You'll be all right," she said, but she didn't look very hopeful and I wondered if I would ever see her again, let alone my family and Marc (*her then-boyfriend, Marc Street*).

But these thoughts were swept away as two ambulance men lifted Francesca off the bed so I could lie there instead.

It was the first time I had seen her since she had been attacked. She was in a complete daze and a paramedic was trying to deal with her cut, which was gaping open from her mouth to her ear.

She lifted her head and, gazing at me with her huge eyes, mouthed: "Miss Potts." I wanted to reach out and love her.

Reena's mum, Surinder, was sitting at the other side of the ambulance. Reena was screaming and her mum, who had also been hit, just sat in complete shock.

The paramedic who dealt with me was very calm, but I knew he must be in a terrible state of shock to attend such an horrendous attack.

I told him I couldn't leave the school until all the children were out of the nursery and that I hadn't told anyone about the children hiding in the dressing-up box.

He assured me that someone would take care of them.

The agony of seeing those precious children in so much pain made the journey to the hospital seem like a lifetime. The noise of the siren is a sound that still scares me whenever I hear it.

I have a vague memory of trying to console the children and tell them that we would be at hospital soon.

It wasn't until a few weeks later that Simon, who drove the ambulance, told my mum that I was chatting to the children as if there was nothing wrong with me.

Apparently I told them that we would go into hospital to get some special plasters and these would make us so much better that we would be back at school in no time.

Eventually the doors were flung open at the A & E department of New Cross Hospital. The staff were waiting and as I was being wheeled in I thought: "This is just like Casualty."

I didn't feel any pain and I didn't feel like crying – until I looked through the gap in the curtains next to me.

Francesca was right op-posite me, lying so still. I could see her little face and I could hear her grandmother crying. A nurse pulled the curtain across and said: "She's going to be fine, Lisa."

The picture of little Ahmed's face flashed into my mind and I asked: "Where's Ahmed?" I was told he must have gone in another ambulance, and I thought: "That's because he's dead and they've taken the dead ones away in another ambulance."

I lay thinking I could have done more and that it should have been me who died. How would I bear it if children had died and I lived?

(*Miraculously, only three children were injured in the attack.*)

I was given some shots to ease the pain but there was still a throbbing in my left arm, a dull pain which remains with me to this day. I'm so used to it now that it's just part of me. But what's a pain for the rest of my life compared to no life at all? I have so much to thank God for.

The nurse helped me into a wheelchair and took me to the bathroom where I looked at myself in the mirror. It didn't look like me.

My hair had been cut away, my head was covered in blood and my back was gaping wide open.

Meanwhile, my mum had arrived and I didn't want her to see me in this state, so the nurse took me back to the cubicle to clean up.

Mum had been called at home and told I'd been injured at school. No details were given to her over the phone, but she'd heard a bit on the radio on the way to hospital, and thought a machete was a gun, and I'd been shot.

She was in complete shock and as white as a sheet when she walked in.

One thing that stands out among the blur of those first hours is my dad's face as he came in. He looked so ill. He'd been mowing the lawn when he got a call telling him to get to the hospital.

He kissed me and then, at last, I was able to tell Mum and Dad what happened.

I drifted off to sleep, and the next time I woke I thought I was at home, and couldn't understand why I felt so weak and couldn't move my arms. I opened my eyes and dis-

covered I was in hospital, with my arms hanging in two stirrups above my head.

Then a nurse came in and I suddenly remembered all that had happened. Immediately I asked how the children were and the nurse said she'd heard they were doing well.

Later I watched TV, and there was my face staring back at me. It was a strange feeling.

As soon as I was able after my surgery I wanted to see the children, and I was wheeled into the children's ward.

There was Reena, playing happily with her brother. She was still hooked up to a drip, like me, but she seemed so cheerful.

As soon as her mum saw me she ran over and kissed me. She kept saying: "Thank you so much, Miss Potts."

Then Reena turned round to see what was going on. She stared at me with her huge, frightened eyes – and started screaming.

What had I done? I'd been so excited about coming to visit Reena, and it upset me terribly that she had reacted to me in this way.

The clinical psychologist

told me later that Reena related some of the attack to me because I was the adult there when it happened.

Yes, I thought, I was the adult, so I should have been protecting the children. They should not have been injured. If only it had been just me.

Yet while I knew that I couldn't have done any more, the "if only, if only" feeling wouldn't go away.

Next I went to see Francesca and wondered how she would react. She didn't cry, but neither did she talk to me. She just stared. Her wound was worse than Reena's, and she'd had a metal plate inserted into her jaw, but she wasn't complaining about the pain.

I visited them each day until they were discharged and they came to visit me to say goodbye. Francesca smiled, but Reena started to cry. I felt so sad, but knew that when I got back to school I could start to work with her slowly. When I left hospital I had another ordeal to face. I was invited to St Luke's to spend an hour with the other staff.

I felt frightened that once I got there I'd relive the whole experience, but I didn't.

The atmosphere was sad and miserable – it seemed as if all the staff were still in shock. It certainly wasn't the happy, buzzing school it had been.

I wanted to go out into the nursery playground, but when I opened the door I saw all the lovely new play surface had been lifted because of the blood on it.

As I stepped out onto the old concrete of the playground I cried for the first time since the attack. This wasn't the nursery I'd loved, it was a dead place where the children and I had been attacked.

But now the court case, which I'd successfully kept at the back of my mind, was nearly upon me. I'd been summoned to appear on Monday, 2 December, 1996.

I wasn't nervous but I couldn't understand why not. I think I expected to take it all in my stride. **"**

Extract 4: *Crazy Horse*

After the Battle

From this distance of years the historians can argue until their teeth rot that one man or another was decisive in this battle, but all these arguments are unprovable now. What's certain is that George Armstrong Custer was very foolish, a glory hound who ignored orders, skipped or disregarded his **reconnaissance**, and charged, all but blindly, into a situation in which, whatever the quality of Indian generalship, he was quickly overwhelmed by numbers.

What I think of when I walk that battleground is dust. Once or twice in my life I rode out with as many as thirty cowboys – I remember the dust that small, unhurried group made. The dust of two thousand milling, charging horses would have been something else altogether; the battleground would soon have been a hell of dust, smoke, shooting, hacking; once the two groups of fighting men closed with one another, visibility could not have been good. Custer received a wound in the breast and one in the temple, either of which would have been fatal. His corpse was neither scalped nor mutilated. Bad Soup, a Hunkpapa, is said to have pointed out Custer's corpse to White Bull. 'There he lies,' he said. 'He thought he was going to be the greatest man in the world. But there he is.'

Most of the poetic remarks that come to us from this battle are the work of writers who

---

reconnaissance checking the position and strength of the enemy interviewed Indians, or those who knew Indians, who thought they remembered Bad Soup saying something, or Half Yellow Face making (probably in sign) the remark about the road we do not know, or Bloody Knife staring long at the sun that morning, knowing that he would not be alive to see it go down behind the hills that evening. All we can conclude now is that Bloody Knife and Bad Soup and Half Yellow Face were right, even if they didn't say the words that have been attributed to them.

Hundreds of commentators, from survivors who fought in the battle to historians who would not be born until long years after the dust had settled in the valley of the Little Bighorn, have developed opinions about scores of issues which remain, in the end, completely **opaque**. Possibly Crazy Horse fought as brilliantly as some think – we will never really know. But he and Sitting Bull and Two Moon survived the battle and Custer didn't. General Grant, no sentimentalist, put the blame for the defeat squarely on Custer, and said so bluntly. The Indians made no serious attempt to root out and destroy Reno, though they could have. Victory over Long Hair was enough; Black Kettle was well revenged.

The next day, to Major Reno's vast relief, the great gathering broke up, the Indians melting away into the sheltering vastness of the plains. . . .

---

opaque unclear

A doomed man

From the day that Crazy Horse came in* he was the focus of rumour, envy, jealousy, and hatred, and it was among his own people that the hatred became a dripping, ultimately fatal poison – a **paradoxical** thing since, except for this short terrible period, no Indian was more respected by the Indian people than he was. Captain John Gregory Bourke, who served with Crook, said that he had never heard an Indian speak of Crazy Horse with anything but respect. And yet, during this one period, the mere fact that the white officers respected him for fighting them so hard in battle made the agency Indians jealous. What they were jealous of, finally, was his moral authority. Among a broken people an unbroken man can only rarely be tolerated – he becomes a too-painful reminder of what the people as a whole had once been.

As I read the records, Crazy Horse at this point was far from being broken, but he was certainly very stressed.

Even though he camped twice as far from Fort Robinson as he was supposed to, he was still in much closer proximity to white people than he had been since his youth on the Platte. He was worried about his people, worried about his wife, and confused by what the whites seemed to want of him. Though there were among the whites men who respected him and some who just liked him,

---

*into the agency run by the whites at Fort Robinson
paradoxical contradictory

he must often have wished that he had continued to hold out. For a time he fidgeted and worried, waiting for the whites to either give him his agency or allow his people to go on the hunt that had been promised.

The whites did neither. Crook pestered Crazy Horse to go to Washington, but Crazy Horse kept backing out. The summer was usually a time of pleasure for the Sioux, but this summer – 1877 – was for Crazy Horse a time of confusion and anxiety.

Meanwhile, the poisons of idleness and jealousy were working on the Sioux. An Indian named Grabber began to spread the rumour that the whites liked Crazy Horse so much that they were going to make him chief of all the Sioux, though at this time he wasn't really chief of any of the Sioux. Jealousy intensified as rumours of his ascendancy multiplied. The whites were as uncertain about him as the Sioux, although one or two experienced officers recognized that he was just off-balance, overwhelmed by his new situation. Too many whites had talked to him too much – and this was an Indian who had never **parleyed** with white men before. He didn't know how to assess the conflicting statements he heard them make.

A few wise officers advised that he be left alone until he calmed down a little and had time to adjust to agency life, but this advice was ignored. Crazy Horse was the star of the hour – everyone wanted to talk to him.

parleyed talked

Extract 5: *War Diaries and Letters*

Letter 1

Camp near Fort Dodge, Kan., Oct. 28, 1868

Day before yesterday a party of Indians made a dash upon some animals **lariated** in the vicinity of Fort Dodge, and succeeded in stampeding and driving off a few horses and ponies, besides doing some other damage, whereupon General Sully wrote a personal letter to General Custer telling him that they 'didn't feel safe at the Post, without some cavalry' and requested that a Troop should be sent up 'to protect them!' It is really amusing isn't it? – when you reflect that there are seven companies of Infantry here, armed with the finest guns in the world, and having in their possession, in addition to their ordinary arms, three or four pieces of Artillery, with men detailed to operate them! General Custer says that he is going to hold onto the letter, to show, if there is any dispute about it, i.e. that the cavalry was wanted here to 'protect' the Infantry! Well, I was sent up yesterday with my Troop, to protect them, and here I am, encamped about three-quarters of a mile below the Post. It has been arranged with General Sully that I am not to report to either the commanding officer of the Post, Major Douglass (3rd Infantry), nor to the commanding officer of the Infantry camp near the Post, Brevet Major Page, 3rd Inf., but am to be entirely independent, and use my own judgment in all cases. I expect to be stationed here until the expedition starts, and will then

---

lariated tethered with ropes

accompany it, in command of a squadron composed of 'G' and 'L' Troops – 'L' Troop is soon to arrive here from Puebla. It is Colonel Sheridan's Troop. A change was recently made in the composition of the squadrons, so that 'I' Troop was put into another squadron. Today it is very windy, and I have seen no Indians yet, and suppose that they will hardly make their appearance until the wind subsides, as they cannot shoot their arrows with much accuracy except when the air is comparatively still.

The Indians who approached nearest the Post the other day were all little boys – only eight or ten years of age it appears! – A large band of warriors, however, was collected in the hills, in rear of the Post, watching them, and ready to make a descent if they had been closely pursued. One of the boys, a son of 'Big Mouth', a noted chief, was wounded by 'Romeo', a half-breed Arapahoe boy who is acting as guide and scout, and who recognized many of the Indians in the attacking party. Romeo's horse was wounded – in the encounter, and he himself made a narrow escape, as his horse fell just as he reached a point from which he was covered by the fire of the Infantry . . .

. . . Concerning all the other columns of cooperation there may be some doubt, but there appears to be no doubt whatever that we are to go down at the appointed time, and spend the winter in harassing the Indians, and in operations calculated to wear down their ponies, so that in the spring – say in March, when their ponies are poorest, we can easily overtake them, and their 'villages' and teach them such a lesson as they will not be likely to forget soon! However the president of the society for the prevention of cruelty to animals might regard the matter, I do not think that any mercy will be shown to the Indians when we overtake them! If we fall into their hands, we expect to be tortured to death, and any that fall into our hands may expect to die very speedily . . .

The fact is, Jennie, there appears to be a premium offered for drunkenness in the army! Almost all the old officers drink a great deal. Indeed I do not know any one except General Hoffman who does not, more or less, and a man is not regarded as sociable who does not keep a sort of open house and have something for his friends to drink, and he has a very small chance of becoming popular with the drinking class, unless he indulges a little himself – in fact, they are rather inclined to regard him with some distrust, I think, as one who may be intolerant of their vices! – At all events, I have observed that about nine out of every ten of those who are selected for staff duty are of the drinking class, and as a consequence are most sociable with those who drink and are always ready to lend their influence to have good companionable fellows selected to fill any position that may become vacant on the staff! What I deduce from all this is, that I am never likely to be selected for any staff duty, but will have the pleasure of riding about on these plains so long as there is an Indian left to cause a feeling of uneasiness along the borders. If that is any consolation, dear, why you may as well avail yourself of it!

I cannot conceal from you that I do become dreadfully discouraged. Not because of the hardships which I endure, and dangers which I undergo, but because of the necessity of being forever separated from you. I dare not tell you how unhappy I am at times, when I think of the dreary prospect. All my philosophy is of no avail, and my only relief is in tears. The companionship of those about me is irksome to me, and I long, oh, with an unutterable longing for the society of my own, dear wife! So wretched do I become, at times, in spite of all efforts to prevent it, that I could wish to die, if it were not a selfish wish.

Letter 2 (dictated)

Washita Battlefield, Nov. 23, 1868

When the appointed moment had arrived, the Regimental Band struck up 'Gari Owen', and the squadrons moved forward with a rush, and all was activity; the Indians were completely taken by surprise. Yet they were instantly up and around. The fighting was severe but I am unable to say how many were killed. The bodies of 103 warriors were found in and around the village, but many more must have been killed whose bodies were carried off by their friends. It was surprising to see how soon, when once the action had commenced, how all the hills were alive with mounted warriors, armed and equipped with their shields, and war bonnets. These, as it was afterwards ascertained, had come from other villages in the valley, having heard the firing. Shortly after the firing commenced I observed a large body of Indians running off towards the left. I at once dashed in among them, passing through a large drove of Squaws and children who were screaming and very much frightened. I came upon the warriors who were ahead and striking out as hard as they could run for their ponies. Riding up close along side of the first I shot him through the heart. He threw up his arms, by the same movement drawing his bow from the scabbard let fly an arrow at me. This was the last act of his existence. I passed on to the second and shot him in the same manner. There was yet another close to me. He was armed with a large Lancaster rifle given to him by the **peace commission**. He took aim, while I was closing upon him and about to fire, but was several times disconcerted by my acting as if I were about to fire upon him myself, until finally I had some doubt if his rifle was loaded. When however I got quite close to him to fire, he returned my fire at the same instant, both shots taking effect. Mine I believe must have passed through his heart, as he threw up his hands frantically and as I was told by others of my company died almost immediately.

I rode back toward the village, being now unable to manage my horse, and the pain of my wound being almost unbearable. I dismounted

---

peace commission guns had been given to Indians in an effort to gain their trust and lay down in such a way that I would not bleed internally. As soon as the fight was nearly decided I was placed upon a buffalo robe and carried down the hills a few hundred yards further, where I was allowed to rest in a place of comparative security until Doctors Lippincott and [William H.] Renicke arrived. Both were so blind, from the effects of snow, that they with difficulty could attend to the wounded, and pronounced my case truly hopeless, but made every effort for my comfort for the short time it was supposed I had to live. All the officers gathered about me, as the progress of the fight permitted, and endeavoured to cheer me with their condolences; in the meantime the Indian village was burned together with a quantity of stores, supplies, gun powder, etc. – and all the ponies that could be gathered together, were driven in. Two were selected for each of the Squaws, who were captured, and two for each officer; the remainder, some eight or nine hundred, were shot to prevent them falling into the hands of the Indians. We now awaited the arrival of our ambulances, which were toiling towards us through the intricate labyrinths where our horses could hardly proceed by file. When at length these arrived the wounded were loaded in, and we commenced our return march towards this point.

Activities

1   In Extract 1, read the accounts of Morrison's visits to the registry office and medical-school library. Each contains narrative and dialogue. Examine the language of the registrar and the librarian in each dialogue. Referring to each woman's use of language, comment on:

    a   what evidence (if any) there is that she is being businesslike

    b   what signs (if any) there are that she is becoming less formal

    c   how appropriate you feel her choice of language is in the situation.

2   Read Extract 2.

    a   Look at the tales told by the three men in the first paragraph. Assume they were once schoolmates, and use what they say as the basis for a short conversation between them in which they swap their stories. You could extend this by adding some food-related tales from your own experience. Write using the layout for direct speech, indicating narrators, and show something of how they expressed themselves and responded to each other. Your spoken version may be less formal than the paragraph in the extract.

    b   Work with another person on the practical matters of providing a meal for yourselves and two friends. Assume you have the use of a well-equipped kitchen with basic ingredients in the cupboards. Using the title 'Our two-course menu for four', make notes under these headings,

which you will use later to present to your class:
  i   Shopping list and budget
  ii   Preparation, timing, who does which tasks
  iii Reasons for your choices

When you listen to the presentations, you could grade them not only on their speaking and listening skills, but also on teamwork, practical matters and the attractiveness of their menus.

c Imagine you were asked to make some closing comments on the programme. Give a brief answer to the presenter's prompt: 'To finish our programme today, here's some advice from one young listener to those responsible for institutional food.'

3 Read Extract 3. Lisa Potts' story has been told in two different forms, in an autobiography and in a series of articles in *The Mirror*. Extract 3 comes from that series.

  a Who worked with her on these two different forms and why do you think she did not write alone?

  b Look at the use of layout in this extract. Obviously *The Mirror* format is larger than this textbook but some of the features of the newspaper article remain: comment on the use of the headline, emboldening, the giant inverted commas, and use of italics. Look at an example of each feature and comment on the effect it has on the reader.

  c Select several paragraphs in this article and count the number of sentences in each. Do the same with Extract 4. What conclusion might you draw about the number of sentences per paragraph in Extract 3 and the reason for this?

4 Read Extract 4.
  a In the first part, what does the writer conclude about historians' and interviewers' accounts of the Battle of the Little Bighorn?
  b Look at the second part of the extract. In this part, the writer tells what happened when the Sioux warrior finally came into the settlement and gave himself up. How did the reputation of Crazy Horse amongst his people change from that time?
  c In the future, the statue of Crazy Horse will become the largest sculpture in the world. It will require an inscription to be chiselled into the mountainside near it. Use the ideas from the extract to write a suitable statement for that inscription. Try to summarize what he meant to the people of his day and suggest what he might mean to people now. Keep to a limit of 50 words.

5 Read Extract 5.
  a In Letter 1, what impression of soldiering would the Captain's wife have had on reading this letter (consider his thoughts on the infantry within Fort Dodge, his fellow army officers, his personal situation and their enemy – the Indians)?
  b In Letter 2, the Captain says people thought his wound was fatal. Look at the language he chooses to dictate this news to his wife. What impression is he trying to create this time? What details during and after the battle does he include to make the situation sound real to her?

6 Read through all the extracts in Section 2. One theme linking the extracts in this section is 'emotion' – the feelings involved as we share things with people, or watch them go through extreme situations. To one individual, a fried egg is his heart's desire! One family feels so strongly about a dead hero that they are determined to carve the world's largest statue of him! Use the title 'My temperament' to describe yourself in terms of what makes you laugh, afraid, angry, relaxed, anxious, sympathetic, etc. If you swap descriptions with a friend, you may be able to give some feedback to him/her on how true-to-life their descriptions seem.

Section 3
Making Connections

Finding an identity is part of understanding ourselves and other people. Going through puberty, making our own circle of friends, developing personal relationships in which we love and are loved – we expect to be involved in all of these activities. Coming into adulthood presents us with many questions, some of which are posed in and around the extracts in this section. How far do we follow the crowd? How much do we count on our family and friends? Are men and women so different that we should consider them separate species? The following extracts look at relationship issues.

Extract 1: from 'Teen Sex? Play the Waiting Game for Best Results' by Hester Lacey, *Independent on Sunday*, 26 July 1998 (page 59)

Is it peer pressure that makes teenagers force their parents to buy expensive clothes so they can feel part of the crowd? We identify with a group of friends, wearing the same clothes, spending leisure time together. We even think along the same lines, and may allow persuasive friends to make decisions for us. David Bull argues that this same urge to be like everyone else persuades some teenagers to try sex before they are ready.

Extract 2: from 'Siblings for Sale!', by Sarah Gill, RANT series, *J17*, July 1998 (page 62)

Those nearest to us are not always dearest. Family friction is nothing new. It happens between generations. When it happens within the same generation, we call it 'sibling rivalry' and here is a 'rant' about that topic. Look out for the non-standard English expressions.

Extract 3: from 'Physical Education', *Sexism in the Secondary Curriculum*, by Pat Browne, Lene Matzen and Janie Whyld (page 63)

Most of you reading this book will be doing so in a mixed-sex classroom. Even though co-education is widespread today, some schools are experimenting with separate-sex teaching in subjects such as science and modern foreign languages in order to raise academic achievement. The pendulum swings backwards and then forwards again. In other schools, providing equal opportunities may involve bringing boys and girls together where traditionally they were separated. This extract looks at the arguments for teaching boys and girls together in PE.

Extract 4: *Aleppo Hamam*, by Angela Barrs (page 69)

The previous extract may have seemed strange to some of us from cultural backgrounds which traditionally separate boys from girls for most activities after puberty. There are occasions we may deliberately choose to be in same-sex groups. There is plenty of enjoyment to be found in activities which keep the sexes apart. My Christmas Eve is not usually spent in the way I describe here but it is a regular event in many Syrian cities, with a separate weekly programme for men and women. The ancient city of Aleppo has a *hamam* similar to the baths the Romans used.

Extract 5: from 'Men are hopeless at talking, say the Samaritans. Women do it too easily. All Agreed? (Just nod for yes)', by John Diamond and Nigella Lawson, *The Observer*, 17 May 1998 (page 73)

Speaking and listening: we know they are important life skills, vital aspects of GCSE English too, but perhaps they are timewasters also. Do men talk with men, and women with women for different purposes and in different ways? Look at both sides of the case . . . and take note of the editor's final comment.

Extract 1: *Teen Sex?*

Teen sex? Play the waiting game for best results

The age of consent should be the same for everybody. But with the benefit of hindsight, would you have been quite so eager to get started? **Hester Lacey** meets the man trying to persuade young people to stay 'cool and celibate' and we urge all virgins to look before they leap . . .

DRINKING, smoking, taking drugs, having sex: all mysterious activities that are forbidden to the young. And so, of course, the ones they rush out most eagerly to experiment with. Trying to demolish the glamorous mystique around these grown-up pastimes is a hideously difficult task;

'While the decision to have sex is a bigger one for girls from the physical point of view, emotionally both boys and girls have a lot to lose'

Dr David Bull, however, has bravely set out to make not having teenage sex into a credible option, in *Cool and Celibate?*, his new book. A veteran of BBC children's

television, where he appears on *Newsround*, *Fully Booked* and *Saturday Aardvark*, he possesses impossibly boyish and twinkly looks, so much so that he makes Philip Schofield look like a grizzled old grandfather. However his television sparkle belies his qualifications: he is in fact Dr Bull MB BSc, BSc ASM. He completed his medical education at St Mary's Hospital in Paddington and worked as a full-time NHS doctor for three years.

Sex, he says, is one of the subjects children ask him about most. 'I spend a great deal of my professional life talking to kids. I look younger than I am, I do very naughty, silly things on television and I don't wear a suit and tie, so kids see me as an older brother. They will ask me things they wouldn't ask a doctor.' The subject, he says, is 'a complete minefield' and he insists he is not setting himself up as a cool role model – 'if you do that, you're heading for a massive fall'.

Cool and Celibate? is, he says, the first book of its kind aimed at teenagers to promote celibacy as a positive state and the first to emphasize the importance of a good relationship over and above its sexual aspect. 'There are a hundred and one books on the mechanics of it all but none about emotions.' He believes that the key to his mission is information, clearly laid out and attractively presented. 'The biggest mistakes come from lack of knowledge, and kids pretend to know more than they do, it's part of growing up. I don't believe in lecturing – I believe in letting children make up their own minds. But knowledge is power. My philosophy is to say decide for yourself, don't be pressured by myths or hype. Think about certain points, then make your own decision.'

He is not the only one to be turning his attention to

'I think it must have been the worst sexual experience of my life; even now I can't think of it without blushing. At least I wasn't actually sick on her'

teenage sex. Last week the House of Lords controversially overturned a parliamentary vote in favour of lowering the homosexual age of consent from 18 to 16 and a NOP opinion poll has shown that only a third of the public support the change. The government is also planning a major campaign against under-age sex, to be launched later this year after under-age pregnancies hit a 10-year high in 1996, the third successive annual rise; the UK has one of the highest rates of under-16 conception in Europe.

But can a book really hope to wield much influence? *Cool and Celibate?* (Element £3.99) is aimed at 12-year-olds upwards. The book takes a fictitious teenage couple, Kerry and Paul; Paul wants sex but Kerry isn't sure. It follows their relationship and takes the opportunity to haul out quite a few issues along the way. It is laid out in the same style as many magazines aimed at this age group; information comes in manageable chunks with plenty of inviting sidebars and boxes and quizzes and checklists, and 'no ridiculous cartoons', says Dr Bull with a wince.

Edward Sutton, 16, gave it his guarded approval. 'It is certainly easy to read and gets the facts across. It is much better than the lessons we had at school. But I think girls would read this kind of thing more than boys.' (He was somewhat nonplussed, however, when asked why girls should be the ones to take more interest. 'In fact,' says Dr Bull, 'while the decision to have sex is a bigger one for girls from the physical point of view, emotionally both boys and girls have a lot to lose from taking the wrong decision'.

... 'I remember just lying there looking at the ceiling, thinking: "Well, is this what it's like? Big deal", says one girl. 'We'd done loads of things before that were much more exciting and lovely, the actual sex was a real anti-climax. As for an orgasm: it took me years after to get that far.'

Boys can equally find the whole experience a damp squib.

'I was terribly drunk and feeling quite ill and as soon as I'd finished I had to leap out of bed to be sick, but I didn't make it to the sink. I think it must have been the worst sexual experience of my life; even now I can't think of it without blushing. At least I wasn't actually sick on her, only on her carpet. Luckily she calmed down enough to be sympathetic afterwards but it could have been enough to put me off for life.'

Doctor Bull offers no guarantees. 'I don't set myself up as some great guru of knowledge, though I can facilitate and communicate. Well, it's all incredibly complicated,' he points out. 'After all, most adults haven't got it right, have they?'

Extract 2: *Siblings for Sale!*

Sure, they're young, they're family and they can even be quite sweet sometimes, but if murder didn't mean a hefty jail sentence I'm pretty sure my little brother and sister would have met with a nasty accident by now. No, I'm not some kinda weird psychopath, but ask anyone with younger sibs what I'm on about and they'll know what I'm saying.

For starters, you have to be constantly on your guard against the 'Please can I borrow . . .' line if you want to keep hold of your wardrobe/CDs/sanity. My sister was after my fave pair of white strappy sandals, and knowing that all she ever does is get into scraps with the boys at school I refused point blank. Of course, she took them anyway and returned them with one strap less and an apologetic expression. When I turned to Mum to back me up, she just came out with, 'Sharing is what sisters are all about.' Aaarrgh!

Another nightmare is that my sister has known me a lot longer than my mates and thinks it's her duty to remind the world I used to kiss the blokes on the posters in my bedroom and swan round the house pretending to be a fairy princess. And when I do confide in my own flesh and blood about my latest crush, she can't wait to point him out to everyone from my mum to my long-lost cousin twice removed. It's her sense of humour. Apparently.

My younger brother isn't any better. He and his silly little friends live to get in my way. They've got nothing better to do than watch me do my *Scream* impression when they throw bangers at my feet or run round me chanting, 'Sarah's got spots!'

HOME ALONE

I thought I'd finally found a use for my little bro' and sis' when Mum and Dad offered me some dosh to babysit them for an evening. Suddenly it all made sense. The torture I'd suffered at their hands would be worth it if I could get the money to see *Titanic* for the seventh time. But not even seeing Leo in his posh evening clobber was worth what I went through. Three hours of tantrums, trashing, screaming and pleading later, Mum and Dad came home to a tip. And who got all the blame? Me.

Mum's sister lives in America and they really miss each other, so Mum's always saying, 'When you're older and living thousands of miles apart, you'll regret all the horrible names you called each other.' But thousands of miles isn't far enough for me.

I sometimes can't help wishing I was an only child. Then I could have all the chocolate cake to myself, I wouldn't have to worry abut Barbie wearing my lipstick, and my pocket money would treble. Sorted. The downside is that I wouldn't have anyone to help entertain dull relatives at family parties or clean my room in return for a read of my *J17*. But hey, I could live with that.

J17 READER SARAH GILL WANTS RID OF HER YOUNGER BROTHER AND SISTER. ANY OFFERS?

SIBLINGS FOR SALE!

Extract 3: *Physical Education*

Until children reach puberty, there are no major physical differences between boys and girls, so there is no physical justification for having certain exercises for girls and others for boys. During and after puberty, changes occur in the body which put boys at a physical advantage. They become able to absorb more oxygen than girls, the amount of muscle in boys represents a higher percentage of their total weight, and they grow bigger than girls. This provides the physiological reasons for the segregation of the sexes, but social expectations of what is appropriate for boys and girls carry far more weight. It should be remembered that statistics relating to the physical development of the sexes refer to the average boy and girl, and there will be many individuals who do not fit this general pattern.

There is often the objection that if PE were mixed, boys, being stronger, would become bored if they were not able to use all their strength, and had to pay attention to the less able (girls) all the time. This is a question of grading exercises, which has to be faced by any teacher of mixed-ability classes. It must be shown, particularly to boys who have undergone 'traditional' sports training, that PE is not only concerned with muscular strength, but also with control and discipline of the body. Taking part in mixed physical activities might well encourage girls to assert themselves more, if the teacher is able to create an atmosphere where girls feel free to develop their physical potential at the same rate as boys. If girls are good at football, there should be no barriers to their joining a team, or forming one of their own. Probably they would gain experience faster by playing in the boys' team in league matches, as has already happened in a London junior school.

Some people enjoy mixed physical activities, and some do not. If the school curriculum allows a choice, so much the better. Schools which already operate mixed games sessions, often find they end up with some mixed and some single-sex activities, simply through pupil choice. A Lincolnshire 11–18 comprehensive has mixed games for fifth- and sixth-formers (compulsory for the fifth, and optional for the sixth, although only half a dozen pupils choose private study instead). Games are chosen each term from soccer, rugby, hockey, netball, badminton, volleyball and basketball. All, in theory, are mixed, but girls are not encouraged by anybody to do soccer or rugby. If a girl wanted to do these, she would be allowed to, but none so far have wanted to. Some arguments are put forward, like 'it would spoil the boys' game', and 'The boys would be afraid to tackle properly'. The Rugby Football Union is unhappy about the insurance against injury for girls. The school would like to run an all-girls soccer option, but at present is restricted by staff shortage. Netball remains all-girls by choice; boys tend to choose basketball. The other games are fairly evenly mixed.

The pupils' reaction to mixed games is 'OK'. 'It appears to them a natural thing to do.' When they first start in the fifth form, there are questions like 'Can boys do hockey?' to which the answer is 'Yes'.

'It's as simple as that.' The girls like mixed hockey. 'Occasionally they complain that a boy is playing like a bull in a china shop. They usually deal with the boy themselves, maybe go over to him and say something like "Watch your stick".' The hockey team is coached by a male teacher. Play has always been aggressive, but now it is more skilful.

At this school, there is also one period of PE each week in single-sex groups. The reason given for this is 'tradition'. Boys and girls are timetabled for PE at the same time, so there would be no practical difficulties in having mixed sessions. There was once a mixed group of first years for PE because of a 'fluke' of timetabling. It was 'all right'. The pupils liked it. The girls were a bit shy at first, but it only took a couple of weeks to get over that. There were no complaints from parents. Boys and girls competed equally. On the whole, boys learnt skills more quickly and reached a 'plateau' of ability, and then, three or four weeks later, the girls would catch up. There was no adverse reaction from the other staff because they were 'only first years'. After discussing the issue of mixed PE the head of PE, a woman, said, 'Your questions are making me think that maybe it's time to get such things discussed at our Curriculum Planning Board'.

Competition or cooperation?

One of the most widely accepted opinions about human nature is that people perform best when motivated, and in our culture motivation is usually provided through competition, which is held to be a natural instinct, and desirable – necessary for survival. We would argue that this is mistaken and that cooperation is more important than competition. People are taught to be competitive; 'Don't cheat' means 'Don't help or ask for help from others'. Competition engenders all sorts of unpleasant feelings, such as being pushy to win, and resentment inevitably accompanies failure.

To accept that people can be motivated without competition, it is necessary to understand the distinction between competition and challenge. Most of the positive effects of competition are, in fact, those of challenge – the thrill of success, managing to achieve something against difficult odds, like climbing a mountain or reaching a personal best time. All of these help to build self-confidence. Whenever there is competition, there is always a loser – and this involves loss of confidence which will only turn into a desire 'to do better next time' if there is a realistic chance of success; the problem is that many people learn early on that they are never likely to win, so give up making any effort whatsoever. Even worse are the unhealthy attitudes engendered in the winners – 'We're the greatest', 'Holier than thou', 'You're not worth bothering with now'. Most school games lessons are geared towards competitive sports, perhaps because hardly any non-competitive games exist in Britain now, although some are being developed or rediscovered.

The present enthusiasm for marathon running is a good example of how a sport can be enjoyable for both participants and spectators, although little emphasis is laid on winning. In the 1981 London Marathon, the two leading runners, Beardsley and Simonsen, made a point of finishing together, holding hands. Spectators regularly show as much interest in and support for those runners who finish against difficult personal odds – the old, the obese, those in weird garb, and those who collapse under the strain but crawl to the finishing post – as in those who finish first. This has encouraged the participation of many who would normally be excluded from competitive sport, where only the best are selected for teams.

All sports which are not team games can be practised in a non-competitive way by laying the emphasis on beating the clock, or improving on a personal or team best. For running over a short distance, each group (or the whole class, if space allows them to run at once) could have their times added together, with the aim of achieving a class record at the end of every lesson. Where pupils are performing the same type of activity, and there is bound to be comparison between personal performances, set different aims for each person, like a handicap race, and make it quite clear that they should be aiming at improving their own performance, and not at beating the person next to them. Group exercises can be designed to require a number of skills which might be provided by different group members: the teacher asks a group to jump a total length of exactly x metres; the last person to jump might not have to jump very far, but very accurately. The teacher's attitude is very important. If the same exercise is set for several groups, and the one which finishes first, or most accurately, is praised, then the exercise becomes competitive.

Extract 4: *Aleppo Hamam*

Aleppo Hamam
5.50 p.m. Christmas Eve, December 1997

1 Late December, biting cold and getting dark. Our small group waits in a short queue outside the building whilst the last few men leave. Sleek limos whisper to a halt alongside us; sombre, cloaked figures slip out, their black wisps of cloth drift past us. Under an arch, a grim-faced man peers into those shadowy faces. The figures melt into the gloom of the interior.

2 What was he looking for? As the hour changed, so did his clients. The men had left the *hamam* and only women, swathed to the eyes, dared meet his gimlet stare. For this was the hour of the women!

3 Inside the cavernous reception hall, surrounded on three sides by a raised platform, divan-style seating waited for us. Recesses fronted by beaded, swinging curtains divided off alcoves where cloaks and headscarves were folded away for sixty minutes. The square ceiling with mini-domes showed navy blue star-shapes of the night sky. Just as it did hundreds of years before, for hundreds of other women.

4 Warmth returned and faces glowed as outer garments were packed away. Everywhere there was frantic action as women emerged like butterflies, in leotards, cozzies and lacy slips. Already the clock had ticked away precious

minutes. Nudity? That was strictly for the children, flinging off their clothes and scampering into the next hall. We could hear their shrieks of laughter echoing around the marble floors. In our hall, every female type was represented: ages, colours and shapes of all sorts. Tiny children too, boys as well as girls, and babies at the breast.

5 Little by little, the hall emptied. We walked towards the fog and warmth of the **tepidarium**. As we moved through the narrow connecting tunnels, water flowed back past us in channels. Water tickled over our bare toes. Water slapped under our flip-flops. From square sinks in each wall, overflowing hot water eddied across the floor into gurgling channels. We copied the regulars, taking brass basins from the sinks and chucking water over ourselves before moving on.

6 A sudden turn and we arrived in the steam of the **caldarium**. Our eyes adjusted to the vast space, the mosaic floor, more little starry domes above. Steam clouds parted to reveal girls' and children's groups sitting round picnicking. As we moved around, grannies offered us tastes of crunchy nut crumble, fiery pastes and smooth dips. The trays held silver and brass bowls with dishes the colours of the

---

tepidarium The name used by Romans for the warm room between the cool and hot rooms in the baths
caldarium The hot room

rainbow. Sour followed by hot, sweet by savoury, we tried them all, laughing and chatting in a mix of English and Arabic. Yells of delight bounced off the walls as naked little ones whizzed past, aquaplaning from mum to mum. Mothers sat in their sopping wet clothes smiling at each other and at their children. In the next much hotter room, we joined a small colony of several women lying like seals on a beach, lapped by the tides. The group resolved itself into the soap queue. In Aleppo, the soap is famous and shops display it in pyramids of dark-green bricks. From laurel and olive trees, it went for centuries on camels across deserts, and now it crosses oceans for tourist souvenirs.

7 Water poured in rivulets off a huge matron in a black petticoat who seized each waiting woman by turn in a neck grip. Our heads were squashed between her enormous breasts and we were loofahed with suds and scalding water. We tourists waited our turn with some trepidation, to be pinioned, soaped and scrubbed. As mine came around, she pointed to her ample bosom and, holding down one thumb, splayed her fingers out proudly to mime for me (as I slid across for soaping) that she had breastfed nine children. I tried to respond with wonder and admiration but my open mouth filled with water. I stopped trying to speak. Two brass bowlfuls of water caught me in the chest as she skidded me across to her colleague for the massage. I slithered to a halt

in the next small room. Alone but for the smiling lady who gently kneaded me half-asleep.

8 Back in the first room, the minutes had ticked away. Dried and dressed, slumped in heaps on divans, we drink pale tea and chat. A beautiful young woman begins to sing as another keeps time on a simple drum made out of skin stretched over a wooden frame. Eyes close as others join the chant. The children sit quietly at their mothers' feet. The cloaks and drapes are brought out. The singing stops. In twos and threes the shrouded figures ebb away. The steam billows out into the frosty night.

Extract 5: *Men are Hopeless at Talking . . .*

Men are hopeless at talking, say the Samaritans. Women do it too easily. All agreed? (Just nod for yes)

He says...
by John Diamond

Let us consider the boozer, which is not to say the man but the place wherein he boozes. I say 'boozer' rather than pub because I specifically don't mean one of the new-style, family-friendly, isn't-it-wonderful-how-a-girl-can-sit-alone-there places, but the places pubs used to be when a lone woman could be frozen out with a stare.

Boozers were the preserve of the male. They served dark and warm male drinks in male quantities and encouraged male games to be played in a fug of male smoke. And there were thousands of them. From where I'm sitting in a fairly anonymous part of West London I can think of a dozen erstwhile boozers, within slouching distance, and there was a time when most evenings they would have been full of men. The men would have been talking to each other about the things men talk about – women, sport, work, music; the things that are the routine stuff of the more oafish sitcoms. The things that men have always talked to their friends about.

For when women used to say in that pitying way that men didn't talk to each other 'properly', what they meant was that they weren't around when men were doing most of the talking. If you draw a graph of the rise of men's groups and lads' mags it will show an increase in inverse proportion to the male boozer's decline.

But if women – and the Samaritans – are wrong

when they say that men can't talk to each other, they're right when they list the things we don't talk about.

We tend, it is true, not to talk about each other. Generally speaking we don't speak ill of our friends behind their backs unless we also think ill of them. After all, why take the piss out of a friend behind his back when you can do it to his face? Nigella talks about slagging off husbands and boyfriends, which is understandable enough in that tedious, Thurberesque battle-of-the-sexes way. But then she goes on to boast that women will say the nastiest things behind the backs of those other women who turn out to be their good friends.

It is this trait which hints at female friendship's dark secret: which is that women are very good at acting friends. They have learned the language of close friendship and speak it as if it were their own – but often with the giveaway perfection of the foreign spy. Give a girl a bust relationship to deal with, a stood-up date, a bereavement, a sacking, and she'll know just what to say, to do. I have seen two women commiserating over one's lost boyfriend in the most intimate terms, and learned later that the two had met just the week before.

It is true, as the Samaritans point out, that we don't know what to do if a male friend cries. 'Three times more men than women would pretend they hadn't noticed if a friend broke down in tears,' says the survey. But the useful question would have been how many men had ever been in that situation and taken that course, because the reality is that men don't break down in tears, or at least not as often as women do.

This may be a bad thing, but it is no reflection on male friendship. We don't know what to do if a male friend cries: it's not something you need that often.

If we did phone up our mates all the time and had the long twittering conversation which even cartoon-strip artists have given up parodying; if we did cry on each other's new shoes all the time, or share beds without a second thought, would we commit fewer suicides? And how happy would that make the Samaritans?

Because it strikes me that the worthy organization is not saving lives but stirring things up. It's one thing to say that 'More than twice more men' (sic) than women think 'people should keep their problems to themselves', but quite another when it turns out that the figures were a mere 7 per cent and 3 per cent respectively.

Just the sort of dodgy statistical tactic a woman would use, don't you think?

She says ...
by Nigella Lawson

Those of us who didn't have the misfortune to be born male can expect and accept any number of comp-liments, these days, purely on grounds of our sex. Being

female is no longer simply our gender but our leading attribute. We're better pupils, better people, better parents, better listeners, better friends. And we've got the statistics to prove it.

I don't deny the force for good – or for survival, which is more important – that is female friendship, but let us not seek canonization for it. Our capacity for friendship – paradoxical though this may sound – stems from our capacity for disloyalty.

No man I know would talk about his girlfriend or wife in the way that women talk about boyfriends and husbands. When women talk among themselves it's not all men, men, men but – in a purely negative way, you understand – that is a great part of it. But more to the point, women talk about each other in the same way.

As contemporary wisdom dictates, we itemize the **puerile** failings of men with scorn for their emotional stuntedness and immaturity; and yet there is something of the playground ethos in female friendship.

Any man would be

---

puerile childish

appalled to hear a couple of women talk of a mutual friend of theirs; it is a given that all will be discussed, nothing is out of bounds. While this is liberating – and, from a post-Diana, let-it-all-hang-out perspective, duly open and **cathartic** – a casual, or merely male, listener might be disconcerted. One night we can be heard talking for hours on the phone with one of our girlfriends, mmming sympathetically to the **litany** of moans – the ungovernable children, the unresponsive boyfriend, the unappreciative boss, the lazy colleagues – the next we're in telephonic **cahoots** with another, not exactly bad-mouthing the first but going over her problems in a way that to the non-initiated might sound very much like it.

But this is not to disparage my own sex. Male loyalty – though I grow to be ever more apprecia-tive of it – is not above suspicion. Men and women deal in different currencies:

within male friendships the

He:

Women speak the language of close friendship with giveaway perfection

currency is status; with women, the currency is vulnerability. (Herein, we shamefully believe or have learnt to believe, lies our sensitivity: and therein our superiority.) Men fear others' pity; women fear others' envy.

No man would want to itemize the many failings of his wife, because to do so would be to risk losing face, losing status. Women, on the other hand, often criticize their men, beyond

She:

A man's girlfriend, wife or family marks the boundary of his emotional existence

even their shortcomings, simply out of fear of seeming smug or lucky or superior. Far from resonating with the

---

cathartic getting rid of pent-up emotions
litany list
cahoots close friendship

self-destructive male fear of self-exposure, we tend, if anything, to be foul-weather friends.

This male reticence may sometimes be misconstrued – perhaps not wilfully, but certainly unfairly, for we benefit. In most couples, it is the woman's friends that become the couple's friends; the man becomes subsumed into her family. But within men's failure to maintain their friendships lies one truth. Far from being emotionally distant from the family, men give their all to it. Maybe we find it a deficient all, but it's true that a man's girlfriend, wife and/or family mark his emotional boundaries. We women retain our detachment, our allegiances to our girlfriends, an emotional life that is not just outside our family but supports, subsidizes it.

Men's failure to expand to fill the emotional space may be counter to modern orthodoxy, but their loss is our gain: can you imagine how undermining it would be if men had the kind of conversations with their friends that we have with ours?

John Diamond and Nigella Lawson never have to talk to each other. They're married.

It's for Real

Activities

1   Read Extract 1 in which Dr David Bull speaks to Hester Lacey about his views on teenage sexual behaviour. Write a blurb about him which might appear inside the back cover of his book *Cool and Celibate?* (The article tells you enough about his background to carry out this task.) Keep the teenage reader in mind and select items from the extract which will make him sound like a writer whose book is worth reading. Keep to a limit of 100 words.

2   Read Extracts 1 and 2. Both extracts use language to persuade people to take a particular view.
    a   Who is the expected reader of each? What makes you think this?
    b   Comment on the use of standard English in each extract: which people use it, and in which situations? Give an example of standard and non-standard language in each extract and say why you think these language choices were made.
    c   Write a paragraph about the vocabulary in these two extracts, commenting on the length of the words chosen and whether you think this has an effect on making the articles easy or difficult to understand.

3   a   Discuss the ideas in Extract 3. Separate them into two lists: pro- and anti-mixed PE lessons in school. (If there are ideas which could belong in either list, put them into a third list.) Which list has the most items in it? Are a large number of minor items more important than a few weighty points?

Draw a line under each of the first two lists and add any of your own ideas. Summarize your discussion using the title: *Separate and mixed-sex PE – our view*.

b Use the title in **a** above to write an essay about PE in mixed or separate-sex groups. You might use the prompts in **a** to plan your essay structure. Notice the title says 'our' view: by all means express your own view but take care to include other views held by your class.

4 Explore the language of Extract 4 in pairs or groups.

a Look closely at paragraphs 1 to 4 describing the exterior and interior of the *hamam*. Note down words or phrases which create an atmosphere or mood *outside*. Then note down those which contrast with them *inside*. What are the differences about?

b Look closely at paragraphs 5 to 7.

i Design a spider diagram with the word WATER in a central circle. Count the number of times it occurs in these paragraphs and add the number next to it. Add any nouns which are used instead of it.

ii Draw a line from the centre to a second large circle. In here put adjectives (or adjective phrases) which describe water.

iii Draw a line out to a third large circle. In here put verbs (or verb phrases) which show actions to do with water.

c Look at the first and final paragraphs. Note down some short quotations involving the idea of *time* from these two paragraphs. How do these words give *structure* to this extract?

d Use the notes from **a**, **b** and **c** to write a short essay about language features used in Extract 4.

5 Read Extract 5 and discuss these questions with girls and boys in your class.
  • Do you often, occasionally or almost never, talk in a single-sex group of friends?
  • Which of these topics would you discuss in a single-sex group: sport, TV, boy/girlfriends, clothes, world problems, your feelings, school, leisure activities?
  • Do you think John Diamond and Nigella Lawson are right about the differences between *what* men and women talk about and *how* they do so?

Write a letter to the editor of *The Observer*, which printed this article. Use the ideas from your discussion and tell the editor whether your group agrees or disagrees with the statement in the title of the article.

6 Read through all the extracts in Section 3. Think back over your early secondary-school years. You had to adjust to new people and friends during a time when you were growing up physically and emotionally very fast. Imagine you have been given the final page in a magazine for readers of 11 to 14 years of age, boys or girls. Write them some encouraging advice from someone who has recently come through those years. Tips on coping with peer pressure, difficult friends or teachers, awkward family situations, girl/boyfriends – what worked for you, or what you learned from bitter experience would be valuable to them. Keep the language light-hearted and remember, this will be the last item they read, and hopefully take to heart.

Section 4
My Place

It seems that we are becoming gradually 'greener'. More and more of us realize that, even as individuals, we have an effect on the world we live in. After all, our homes are connected to services which come in from the outside and the boundary between our home and our surroundings is quite a blurred one. Along with our rights come responsibilities as citizens. Recycling waste and conserving water have become important ways in which each of us can help our communities.

This section begins with a look inside one person's home and contents. He tells us what makes his place important to him. From there, the extracts go on to consider several ways in which the individual's home connects with their neighbourhood. The leaflets from which the extracts are taken deal with our homes and our local environment and how we can care for them.

Extract 1: from 'In Residence: Mark Morriss, *Select – Music and Beyond*, September 1998 (page 83)

A Buddhist monk interviewed about his lifestyle was asked how many vehicles he owned. He replied that he had two – his (only pair of) shoes. By contrast, many of us may be proud owners of all kinds of possessions, some of which we show off happily. Whether you flaunt your property, showy clothes and gadgets, or store them out of sight, your home tells the world something about you. In this magazine article, a celebrity of the day offers readers a 'tour' of his home and collection.

Extract 2: from *Neighbour Noise Problems: What You Can Do*, National Society for Clean Air and Environmental Protection (page 86)

This extract is from a leaflet giving advice on what to do about noisy neighbours.

Extract 3: from *Air Pollution – What it Means for your Health*, Department of the Environment, Transport and the Regions (page 89)

Everyone wants their personal and communal space to be pleasant to live in. Clean air is one of the most basic of human needs.

Extract 4: from *Floodline: Flooding Can Happen to You*, The Environment Agency (page 92)

This information pack stresses how important it is for you to do as much as you can to protect yourself and your property in the event of flooding.

Extract 5: from *Treesponsibility – climate action in Calderdale*, Treesponsibility (page 93)

This small pamphlet shows one active way of improving the local environment, not just for yourself but for others now and in the future. Although all such groups want finance, your time and effort can be as valuable to them as money.

Extract 1: *In Residence*

MARK MORRISS

Several hundred alphabetically arranged videos, over 100 plastic frogs, and a smattering of Star Wars memorabilia . . .
'I'm not anal' says the Bluetones crooner. Hmm . . .

In comfortable proximity to 'London's No 1 Disco Shop' is the modest top floor flat owned and occupied by Bluetones singer Mark Morriss. His home for two years now, this compact space is a shrine to the wonders of visual entertainment, with televisions forming the focal point of both the bedroom and sitting room, and several hundred pre-recorded videos lining the walls.

The décor is understated but attractive, that of a man in touch with his feminine side yet still loath to stack the bathroom with an unnecessary volume of 'products'. Framed David Bailey shots claim the wall-space not yet studded with alphabetized videos. 'They're not like "Aa, Ab"' Mark says defensively, lest he appears too trainspottery. 'They're just all the As, all the Bs . . . I do have to rearrange them all every few weeks to fit all the new ones in,' he sighs. A Herculean task in the circumstances.

Turning the volume down on Cartoon Network to make conversation possible, Mark takes a heavy toke and the guided tour begins . . .

---

1 AT-AT
'I've spent most of my adult life trying to buy back all the things I was forced to give away in my childhood. My brother and myself were forced to give all our *Star Wars* toys away to our cousins who live in South Africa because we were deemed "too old", so we've since spent a small fortune trying to buy it all back. It's really a major part of a lot of people's childhoods. You made friends with people you wouldn't normally have made friends with because you had a *Star Wars* connection. It's a unifying force. Perhaps this was "The Force" everyone was talking about.'

---

2 BRONZE BILL SHANKLY STATUETTE
'He was a big inspiration of mine when I was a young boy. He died when I was young and I remember that, even though I lived in London, his death had a big impact on a lot of football supporters and kids at my school. He's one of those people who was a very simple man with simple values, but when he spoke he always spoke from the heart and had the ability to inspire people to better themselves. A lot of his philosophies about the way you approach football can be applied to life, being true to yourself and trusting in other people.'

3 PLASTIC FROG THAT CROAKS

'I've had an affinity with frogs since as far back as I can remember. When I last had a count I had in the region of 120 different types of frogs, I can't explain why. There's something very comforting about their big eyes and smooth skin, that sort of thing. I just find them very satisfying to watch. It's not all amphibious creatures, just frogs. The smoother the better.'

4 VIDEOS

'I started collecting about ten years ago, maybe more. The first video I bought was "Arena" by Duran Duran. I know exactly how many I've got: 671! I'll go away for a few months and when I come back I go and buy five or six videos in one big heap. People always buy me videos for birthdays and Christmas. I'm a big collector of stuff so I like to get the whole set of things. I like the first two *Robocop* films, for example, but I've got to get the third one even though it's crap just to get the set. I've got all of Stanley Kubrick's films and all of Woody Allen's films. I've got three *Star Wars* trilogies because they keep improving 'em! I really like watching movies, good or bad. Some of my stuff really stinks but it's stuff that I have a personal affection for. They're all in together, though, out and proud.'

5 SIMPSONS TOYS

'I've become a bit of a *Simpsons* obsessive in the last year and a half, since getting cable. Being off the road a lot last year and in the studio, I watched a lot more television and caught up with a lot of things I'd missed from being so busy. *The Simpsons* is easily the most subversive programme on telly. I mean, the accusations it makes against the American Government week in, week out, taking the mick out of any nationality be it English, Japanese, Pakistani, and getting away with it because it's a cartoon . . .'

6 TELESCOPE
'Because this is a top floor flat, in the summer when the sky's really clear you can get a really good view of the moon. It looks different all the time, some nights you can see amazing things, valleys and that. It used to belong to my girlfriend and she didn't use it any more so she let me have it. I can climb out onto the roof and set it up, go out with my ghetto blaster and have a smoke and look at the moon.'

7 SIGNED LIVERPOOL SHIRT
'We made friends with this guy who works at Anfield on the door to the players' lounge and dressing rooms, and I got his kids tickets for gigs whenever we played in or around Liverpool. To say thank you he gave me a signed Liverpool shirt at the end of last season. I was well made up. When I was growing up my stepdad was Scottish and at the time Kenny Dalglish, Alan Hansen and Graeme Souness were all playing for Liverpool, so when he came to live in England he started supporting Liverpool. I inherited that when I was too young to realize the stick I'd get for it later on.'

8 ULTRAMAN GUITAR
'We all bought miniature guitars on our last trip to Japan and this one was the most grotesque one in the shop. I had to have it. Ultraman is a really big superhero in Japan, he frequently saves the Earth from alien invasion. He's like Superman but better; he's got a cooler suit. He grows in size, he flies, he's got laser rays. There's a whole family of these *Ultraman* characters, you can get Ultramum and Ultradad and Ultrabrother and Ultrasister. I just thought that an Ultraman guitar had to be the ultimate collector's piece, really. Ultraguitar!'

9 STAR CHART
'That was a gift from my girlfriend for my birthday last year. She named a star after me, and this has the latitude and longitude of where it is. "Big Mo", it's called. A very sweet thought. I've never been able to find it. I've got all the maps and charts of where it is but constellations are all Greek to me. All I know is there's some corner of the galaxy that is for ever "Big Mo".'

Extract 2: *Neighbour Noise Problems*

One of a series of information
leaflets on environmental issues
produced by the NATIONAL
SOCIETY FOR CLEAN AIR
AND ENVIRONMENTAL
PROTECTION

NEIGHBOUR NOISE PROBLEMS

WHAT YOU CAN DO

Noise from neighbours is a common source of nuisance, and for some people it can be very upsetting. The main problems are caused by barking dogs, loud music or TV, shouting, banging doors and DIY activities. Remember that no house or flat is totally soundproof – everyone can expect a degree of noise from neighbours. If you are being disturbed by noise from neighbours there could be three reasons:

• the neighbours may be behaving unreasonably, for instance by playing loud music late at night or allowing their dog to bark all day.

• the neighbours may be behaving normally, but the sound insulation in the floors or walls between you may not be good enough to cut out the sounds of everyday living.

• you may have become over-sensitive to the noise, particularly if you don't get on with your neighbours. Some people will 'tune in' to the noise from next door and find it annoying even when most other people wouldn't.

What can you do?

Firstly, approach your neighbour and explain politely that you are being troubled by the noise. Although you may find this difficult it is surprising how often neighbours are unaware of the unhappiness they are causing. Most will be glad to do what they can to reduce the noise and may even thank you for letting them know!

If the problem seems to be inadequate sound insulation, there are a number of DIY solutions. A leaflet called 'Improving sound insulation in your home' is available from the Building Research Establishment, Garston, Watford WD2 7JR, price £2 (including postage). You could ask a builder to undertake the work using the BRE guidelines, although you might also wish to seek professional help to determine what work is required and to undertake proper supervision of the work.

If you live in a council property it is worth discussing your problem with the housing department. Most Conditions of Tenancy include a requirement that tenants do not cause nuisance to neighbours; a local authority may be prepared to take action if serious nuisance is being caused.

If your neighbour continues to cause a nuisance you should write to them explaining about the effect the noise is having upon you. Ask them to stop making a noise nuisance, referring to any conversations you may have had and what, if anything, he or she agreed to do about it. Keep a copy of the letter. Start a diary recording the dates and times of any noise nuisance, what the noise was, the effects it has on you, and keep a record of any conversations you have or letters you write.

The pamphlet then goes on to describe action the council can take and how you can take legal action yourself. It finishes with these words:

Legal action is unpleasant and will inevitably further sour the relationship between you and your neighbour. It is very important that you do your best to resolve the problem in a friendly way – legal action should be a last resort. Some areas have mediation services which can help you to resolve neighbour noise problems. To find out if there is one near you contact: Mediation UK, 82a Gloucester Road, Bishopston, Bristol BS7 8BN Tel: 0272 241234

Published by NSCA
136 North Street, Brighton, BN1 1RG
Tel: 01273 326313   Fax: 01273 735802   email: info@nsca.org.uk
http://www3.mistral.co.uk/cleanair

Extract 3: *Air Pollution*

THE AIR POLLUTION BANDS

The Air Pollution Information Service uses four bands to describe levels of pollution. The bands are low, moderate, high and very high.

Healthy people do not normally notice any effects from air pollution, except occasionally when air pollution is 'very high'.

The table below shows the four bands and their impact on the health of people who are sensitive to air pollution.

Pollution Band	Health Impact
LOW	*Effects are unlikely to be noticed even by people who know they are sensitive to air pollutants.*
MODERATE	*Mild effects are unlikely to require action but may be noticed by sensitive people.*
HIGH	*Sensitive people may notice significant effects and may have to take action to reduce or avoid them (for example by reducing time spent outdoors). Asthmatics will find that their 'reliever' inhaler is likely to reverse the effects of pollution on their lungs.*
VERY HIGH	*The effects on sensitive people, described for high levels of pollution, may worsen.*

Sensitive individuals are those people who suffer from heart and lung diseases, including asthma, particularly if they are elderly.

The changes from band to band do not represent sudden steps. The effects of air pollutants on health increase gradually as air pollution levels rise.

It is important to look at the bands in the light of personal experience. Individual people – especially those who are sensitive to pollution – will learn from experience how air pollution affects them. Effects may still be noticed for some days after pollution levels have fallen to low or moderate levels. People with heart conditions or severe lung diseases (e.g. chronic bronchitis or emphysema) may be more sensitive to changes in air pollution than the descriptions suggest. If you suffer from a heart condition and you notice a change in your symptoms get medical advice as you normally would. Do not try to change your treatment yourself.

The Information Service only provides information about the short-term health effects of certain air pollutants. Air pollution is likely to have an effect on health over the longer term, but at the moment we do not fully understand these effects.

POLLUTANTS

The air pollutants which are included in the 'banding' system are nitrogen dioxide, sulphur dioxide, ozone, fine particles and carbon monoxide. With the exception of carbon monoxide, all irritate the lungs and cause inflammation. This means that people who suffer from lung disease may feel less well than usual. In some cases, symptoms may increase to such an extent that a change in treatment, or admission to hospital, may be needed.

THE HEALTH IMPACT

If your health is good, the air pollution we usually get in the UK is unlikely to have any serious short-term effects. That said, on the rare occasions when air pollution levels are very high, some people may feel eye irritation, you may start to cough and breathing deeply may hurt.

However, people with lung diseases or heart conditions are at greater risk especially if they are elderly. Daily changes in air pollution trigger increased admissions to hospital and contribute to the premature death of those who are seriously ill.

Asthma
There is little evidence that air pollution itself causes asthma. However, if you already have asthma, you may find that air pollution triggers an attack, although infections and allergens are more likely to do so.

Smoking
Smoking is likely to have a much more serious effect on your health than air pollution. Giving up smoking will cut down your risk of lung and heart disease considerably. It will also make you less vulnerable to the short-term effects of air pollution.

In winter
If traffic fumes make breathing harder, avoid busy streets as much as you can.

If you are elderly, stay indoors as much as possible and keep warm.

In summer
If you find it harder to breathe on hot sunny days, avoid energetic outdoor activities, especially in the afternoons when pollution levels tend to be higher.

Extract 4: *Floodline*

FLOODLINE
Flooding Can Happen to You

Flooding is an unfortunate fact of life. The Environment Agency aims to warn of river and coastal flooding wherever possible. Your local council and the emergency services may give assistance. *But the person who can do most to help in a flood is you.*

In April 1998 flooding caused insured and uninsured losses of up to £400 million.

In October 1998 an area the size of North Yorkshire was flooded . . . The River Wye at Hereford was 18ft 6in above its winter level.

'We just woke up and heard fire engine sirens outside. We looked out, and the garden had completely disappeared. Then we came downstairs and it was just pouring in.'

'I have seen some floods in my time in the town but this is certainly a bad one. Bits of the place that were submerged are slowly starting to reappear but they could disappear just as quickly with more heavy rain.'

Do take the following steps as soon as you hear a warning. Don't wait until the situation gets worse before you do anything.

DO:
- **Do watch what's happening.** Is the weather getting worse? What are other people doing? Should you be doing the same?
- **Do check on your neighbours.** Do they need your help? Someone near you may not be able to escape upstairs. Or they may be unable to move furniture on their own.
- **Do block doors and airbricks with sandbags or floodboards.** If you cannot get hold of sandbags through your local council, improvise by filling old pillow cases or carrier bags with earth or sand.
- **Do try and keep things warm and dry.** A flood can last longer than you think and it can get cold. Take some warm clothes and blankets upstairs or to a safe place. Take a thermos and food supplies too.

DON'T:
- **Don't leave valuable items where they might be damaged.** Pile up furniture if you can and put valuable items like photographs or electrical equipment up high too. Tie up your curtains and roll up your carpets if you can.
- **Don't leave power supplies on.** Turn off the electricity and gas at the first sign of flooding to your property.

Extract 5: *Climate Action in Calderdale*

Treesponsibility
climate action in Calderdale

Together we can 'green up Calderdale' and safeguard our children's future

F licking a switch or jumping into a car is simple and convenient. It is much harder to face the fact that these everyday activities are changing the climate. Burning fossil fuels provides us with electricity, warmth and transport. But it also leads to carbon dioxide (CO_2) pollution. This will remain in the atmosphere for the next 100 years, 'turning up the earth's thermostat' by adding to the natural greenhouse effect. Nobody knows for sure what the results will be. We do know that they will be irreversible within a lifetime.

That's the problem. If you want to be part of the solution, please read on . . .

Treesponsibility is about caring for the future by taking responsibility for our own CO_2 pollution . . .

. . . and to do that we have to find out what it is. Please spare a little time and effort to work out the amount of emissions from your household using the six steps outlined below. You will need: a calculator and the past year's gas and electric bills.

Step 1
KWH on your gas bills x 0.2 =   _____ Kg CO_2
Units on your electricity bill x 0.9 =   _____ Kg CO_2

Step 2
Estimate how many Kg of coal and
bottled gas you used last year x 3.0 =   _____ Kg CO_2

Step 3
Estimate how many Kg of wood
you burned last year x 1.5 =   _____ Kg CO_2

Step 4

Estimate how many litres of petrol you used last year
(30 miles per gallon = 0.15 litre per mile. Average
yearly mileage is about 12,000)

Each litre of petrol x 2.3 = _____ Kg CO_2
Each litre of diesel x 2.7 = _____ Kg CO_2

Step 5

Estimate how many airmiles
you flew last year x 0.4 = _____ Kg CO_2

Step 6

Add all the figures so far
and divide by 1000 = _____ tonnes CO_2

*We can repay our 'carbon commitment'
by planting trees which draw CO_2 from
the air as they grow*

Although it is impossible to reach a precise formula, every
3–5 trees planted will 'fix' about one tonne of CO_2 over
time.

Planting trees has other benefits too. Trees purify the
air we breathe and nourish the soil. They provide
shade, shelter and a habitat for birds and other
woodland creatures.

Calderdale has lost nearly 90 per cent of its tree cover over
the past millennium. We can reverse that trend and leave a
legacy of beauty for our children and grandchildren.

If you would like to be part of *Treesponsibility*, please turn
overleaf . . .

... and next year?

If you've read this far, you may have already taken the time to work out your household's CO_2 pollution for the past year and decided to repay this 'carbon commitment' by taking part in TREESPONSIBILITY. If so, thank you.

Compensating for our own pollution is good; it's better still to pollute less, in the first place. Saving energy is good for the planet, and good for your pocket . . .

• Turning down central heating thermostats by one degree could cut your heating costs by up to 10 per cent.

• Energy-efficient light bulbs use a quarter of the power of conventional bulbs and last up to eight times as long.

• Fuel bills can be slashed by simple measures like keeping doors shut, turning lights off, not overfilling kettles, unplugging the television at night, and showering instead of bathing.

• Insulating your home makes for more efficient energy use. If you are on benefits, grants are available. A discount scheme is also available, covering every household in Calderdale – contact the Council's Winter Warmer Scheme on 0800 072 0152.

• Buying energy-efficient appliances or vehicles may cost a little more at first, but will save money and energy later on.

• Walking or cycling for short journeys is healthier for you and healthier for the planet.

• Shopping locally will cut down on transport, and benefit your local community.

• Use public transport whenever you can, and cut out unnecessary car journeys.

• If you have to drive, share your car whenever possible.

This leaflet was produced by:
Treesponsibility • 10 Broughton Street • Hebden Bridge • HX7 8JY

Treesponsibility is a cooperative project with support and involvement from: the Green Business Network, the Million Trees Project, Knott Wood Coppicers, Calderdale Council's Agenda 21 process, the Hebden Bridge Woodland Group, the British Trust for Conservation Volunteers and Southall's Trust.

If you'd like to get involved too, please tick the relevant boxes below:

◯ I/we would like to plant _____ trees. Please send me details of times, dates and venues. NB The tree-planting season ends in April and begins in October.

◯ I/we would like to sponsor _____ trees at a cost of £1 per tree. Members of Calderdale LETS Scheme can pay in local currency.

◯ I/we would like to organize a fund-raising tree-planting event for my youth/school/community group/voluntary organization. Please send a free information sheet.

◯ I/we would like to receive the *Treesponsibility* newsletter. I enclose £3.00 for one year's subscription.

◯ I/we would like to make an additional donation of £ _____

◯ I/we can help *Treesponsibility* by distributing leaflets and posters locally.

Name

Address

Telephone

I/we enclose a cheque for the sum of £ _____ made out to 'Treesponsibility'.

Please send this form with a S.A.E. to: *Treesponsibility* • 10 Broughton Street • Hebden Bridge • HX7 8JY

Activities

1   Read Extract 1 introducing you to Mark Morriss'
home and possessions. Imagine you are a celebrity
who is often in the news. You are raising funds for a
charity by allowing the public to visit your home
and look at your personal possessions. Write the
'Visitor's Guide' which the public refer to as they
tour your home and possessions. You will need to
make it friendly, probably exaggerated and maybe
humorous. It could be part of the greatest tourist
attraction in your area. As there is an entry fee,
your tour had better sound worth it.

2   Read Extracts 1 and 2. Take particular note of
Mark's comments on item 6 in the first extract. You
are a person occupying a top-floor flat directly
opposite Mark Morriss. On warm evenings you like
to sit outside on the roof to enjoy the view and to
read the newspaper quietly. Write the script for a
conversation between you and Mark in which you
tactfully explain how disturbing you find his music
outdoors. Take note of the points in Extract 2. The
aim of this dialogue is to remain neighbourly and
try to resolve the difficulty.

3   Read the information from Extract 3. You work for
the DETR and have been asked to design a poster
to display in health centres and libraries to draw
attention to our need for clean air. Select only the
points required to make clear which people are at
risk from air pollution and what they should do to
help themselves. Choose an eye-catching title and set
out your poster as concisely and clearly as possible.

You may visit the following websites and decide whether they provide useful information. *If* you think they do, add the web addresses in small print somewhere on your poster.

1   http://www.environment.detr.gov.uk/airq/aqinfo.htm

2   http://www.doh.gov.uk/hef/airpol/airpolh.htm

4   Read Extract 4. Use these fictionalized details. You live on the first floor of a block of flats overlooking the River Speedwell. The flats seem empty apart from yours and your disabled neighbour's on the ground floor below you. It has been raining heavily all day and the river is beginning to flow over its banks. At four o'clock, you see a flood warning and emergency rescue services number for your area on teletext. Acting on the advice given on-screen, which includes the *Dos* and *Don'ts* from Extract 4, you visit your neighbour and give the help suggested. Then you call the number provided. Use the following starting point for continuing this telephone conversation:

> Rescue services officer: *Hello, rescue services. Can I help you?*

Explain what you have already done to help and give the information the officer asks for. Invent other details you may need.

5   Read Extracts 3 and 5 again and use the ideas to write an article for publication in a local newspaper. You should focus attention on some ways in which you and their readers can actively promote a clean and healthy environment for future generations. Use the title: *A Bright Future for . . .*, putting in the name of an area which means a lot to you, perhaps in your neighbourhood. You *might* follow the plan below. Make your readers feel they want to be involved with the ideas you put forward.

- *Begin* by telling them why the area means a lot to you
- *Continue* by describing one or two aspects which you feel need to be improved
- *Explain* what you and they could do to participate in that change – a brief plan of your ideas (who needs to be involved, what resources would be needed and how the change could be brought about)
- *Involve your readers* by summarizing the important points at the end. This might include a slogan, some contact details or a request for help from them.

6 Read through all the extracts in Section 4. They all deal with places.

   a Draw up a list of ten features of an imaginary city or country area, with some hints about its geography, inhabitants, activities, visual appearance. Give your place a name. When completed, these will be collected and redistributed so that for **b**, you will use a list drawn up by someone else. Make your list interesting: don't make it impossible.

   b Use the list you are given to write a paragraph under the title *A Day in the City of . . .* or *Countryside around . . .* You do not have to use all of the features listed, but use enough of them to make the place as real as you can.

Section 5

Citizens of the World

The first section of this book included extracts about childhood and the effects of time on us. This last section is about working together to make people's lives better, both locally and globally. It begins with some reflections on the upbringing of several Northern Irish children, some of whose adult lives were cut short.

Extract 1: from 'Winners who lost everything', by Fergal Keane, *The Guardian*, 9 January 1999 (page 103)

In this newspaper article, the journalist Fergal Keane talks to Belfast men who remember a brief togetherness in a football team, despite their different upbringings.

Extract 2: from an interview with Rachel O'Connor (page 110)

Rachel O'Connor, now in her early twenties, was completing her training to become a secondary English teacher when she spoke to me about her memories of a Belfast childhood and her hopes for the future. The photograph shows her with a group of sixth-formers from the school she went on to work in.

Extract 3: an advertisement for Christian Aid (page 114)

Being part of a group with a common purpose is rewarding emotionally. It may involve giving up precious time or money but the communal effort is important in itself for many people. Charities can be small and local, or stretch their efforts across the world. In the advertisement which follows, the football image comes up again as we are asked to be part of a worldwide team.

Extract 4: from *Speaking Out: Black Girls in Britain*, edited by Audrey Osler (page 115)

In this extract, some Year 10 Muslim teenagers from Birmingham express their feelings on worldwide issues.

Extract 5: from an advertisement for Oxfam (page 119)

Paul, in the final extract, says, 'my work doesn't take me far'. He may not go far from home, but he feels involved and connected with people across the world.

Extract 1: *Winners Who Lost Everything*

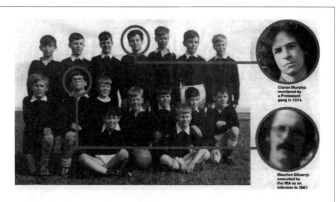

Ciaran Murphy: murdered by a Protestant gang in 1974

Maurice Gilvarry: executed by the IRA as an informer in 1981

In 1968 these Belfast boys discovered team spirit, becoming champions. But in Northern Ireland, it couldn't last. **Fergal Keane** reports on the tragic stories behind this faded photograph.

Winners who lost everything

1   **A** s Joe Skelly remembers, it was a hot afternoon in early summer. The boys in the Holy Cross intermediate Gaelic football team were getting ready for the game when Mr Grogan called them over. Pat Grogan was their teacher and coach, a strong man with a quick sense of humour. The boys liked him. He made them feel like winners, not a bunch of awkward 11-year-olds. That afternoon they'd seen him hauling a large blue bag to the edge of the football field.

2   The boys were dressed in their usual exotic mix of jerseys, most of them hand-me-downs from older brothers, a frayed collage of different colours and

sizes. A proper team kit was out of the question. In the Ardoyne of the late sixties, unemployment was **endemic**. The boys' families had more to worry about than football kits.

3   'Where do you think you lot are goin'?' asked Grogan. 'We're goin' to play the match, sir,' one of them replied. Grogan told them to stand where they were. He opened the big blue bag and reached inside. He began to pull out some football shirts. They were black and white, the colours of Holy Cross Primary school. Grogan handed the jerseys to the astonished youngsters.

4   'Well, yez can't play without a proper kit. Ye can't be winners if you don't look the part,' he said. Thirty years later, sitting in the front room of his terraced house in Ardoyne, Joe Skelly's face lights up when he describes the moment.

5   'We all looked at each other. You know, we were amazed. It was like putting an international shirt on your back. It was absolutely fantastic. We thought we were going to be the superstars of tomorrow, like we really had it in us to be winners. The teacher told us we had it in us.'

6   Grogan lined the boys up for a photograph in their new kit. For many it was their first experience of standing in front of a camera. Another teacher, Cyril Murray, took the photograph. Three decades on, we see them staring earnestly at the camera, mindful of their teacher's exhortation to look like winners and not a gang of giddy boys. But in a few short years, the team would be torn apart by the bitter realities of Northern Ireland's **sectarian** hatred.

7   May 1968, and the world is in turmoil. This is the year of revolution and murder, the time of the street-

---

endemic constantly present
sectarian concerning sects or groups (here, Catholics and Protestants)

fighting man. Ulster's Catholics began to agitate for civil rights. After forty years of discrimination and exclusion, they wanted a fair share of jobs and houses, an end to the **gerrymandering** of local government and reform of the police. But the boys of Holy Cross Primary were untouched.

8   Later that year they won the Belfast Intermediate League. Winners! There was a cup. There were medals. The school went wild with excitement. The players were hailed as local heroes. 'We were the boys that summer all right, we were the boys,' says Joe Skelly. He remembers a team of fairly mixed talent.

9   There were a few real stars like Seamus Clarke and big Ciaran Murphy and Maurice Gilvarry. Tough boys on the field but relaxed and easy-going once the final whistle went.

10   Ciaran's older brother Pat was one of the best players in the district, an all-rounder who excelled at Gaelic football and soccer. He and Ciaran were inseparable. As Pat remembers, they were more best friends than brothers.

11   Being the older of the two, Pat was detailed to take care of his younger brother. Growing up in the two-bedroomed terraced house, they had shared the same bed. When Pat produces the family photograph album, you notice that he is never pictured without his smaller brother: the two boys dressed as cowboys; the two of them playing in the yard. 'He was an original, you know, a big lump of a lad,' recalls Pat.

12   The Murphys lived near and knew the Gilvarry family. With 12,000 people crammed into an area of barely half a square mile, chances are everybody will know everybody else. Pat remembers Maurice as a very quiet individual. He was a bit of a loner, he says.

---

gerrymandering rearranging voting districts in the interests of one party

There were eleven Gilvarrys, crammed into a two-bedroomed house. This was not untypical of Catholic families of the period.

13   Ask Eamon about his brother and football and he smiles. Eamon played for the team as well, but was never good enough to make the final side. His brother Maurice, he says, was skilful but short-sighted. He was good around the field but could be disastrous near the goal. 'God, it was funny,' Eamon remembers. But the days of laughter were to disappear in the spring and summer of 1969. The boys still trained and played. Pat Grogan urged them on to greater glory. But as the civil rights agitation continued, sectarian tension escalated. Going to and from football training was becoming hazardous.

'Had they been brought up anywhere else they would have gotten jobs or gone on to university. But their whole lives were restricted.'

----

14   Ardoyne was largely surrounded by loyalist territory. To the west the Shankill Road, to the north and east the Upper Crumlin Road and Ballysillan. The pitch the boys used for training was smack in the heart of Ballysillan. Sectarian name-calling and skirmishing with the Protestants became a regular occurrence. And then in August 1969 the balloon went up, with Protestant mobs laying siege to Catholic ghettos in Belfast. There were pitched battles in Derry. Ardoyne came under attack with rows of houses burned down and hundreds of people forced to flee the district. Eamon Gilvarry remembers: 'You just never slept. I mean you knew what was going on outside. There was a lot of shooting and I remember

the taste of the CS gas. It didn't sink in, though, until you read the paper. I remember seeing that on the 14th or 15th of August a man sitting in his house here had been shot by the police. That's when it hit you, when you knew how serious it was.'

15 The neighbourhood organized its own defence. Buses were hijacked and placed across the narrow streets. Maurice and Eamon Gilvarry, Pat and Ciaran Murphy, Joe Skelly and Seamus Clarke – all joined in the rioting. Pat Murphy says that in the beginning they were caught up in the excitement and fear. Football had been overtaken by the more pressing need to defend the neighbourhood.

16 One of his strongest memories is of watching a group of young men running across waste ground while snipers were firing at them. The fleeing group were holding a piece of corrugated tin over their heads – useless if the snipers managed to find their range. Luckily the gunmen were bad shots. 'It shows how naïve we were about firearms and what they could do to you,' he says.

17 Some of the football team moved away with their families. Others, like the Skellys and Clarkes and Gilvarrys, stayed. For a short time Ciaran Murphy and his mother emigrated to America. But the call of home proved too strong. It was a fateful return.

18 Pat Murphy still struggles with the memory of what happened to Ciaran. One night in 1974, the big footballer was walking home along Cliftonville Road, about ten minutes from his home, when a car pulled up. There was a struggle and Ciaran was dragged inside.

19 The facts, barely adequate to describe the horror, come from police records: a young Catholic male stabbed repeatedly, shot several times in the face and body, then dumped in a bloody heap on the mountains overlooking Ardoyne. A random victim.

The teacher who took the team photograph, Cyril Murray, was another, shot dead at his home by the UVF.

20   The nature of the conflict changed over the years. The Army came in. The IRA reappeared. Riots gave way to gun battles. Bombs were exploding all over the city. To the British army and police, Ardoyne was IRA territory, a place where soldiers were ambushed and killed.

21   Bitterness was deepening. Tom Dore, a soft-spoken teacher from County Limerick, remembers giving religious instruction classes to the boys from Holy Cross while the streets outside erupted. 'They were young fellows on the threshold of life and had they been brought up anywhere else they would have gotten jobs or gone on to university. But their whole lives were restricted. They couldn't travel outside their own area. They had to survive. I tried to preach the gospel of forgiveness, but I often felt I was getting nowhere.'

22   Tom has fond memories of one member of the team, Seamus Clarke. 'He was a fantastic fellow. If I had bet on anything it would have been that he might have become a bishop or something.' Instead Seamus became a leading IRA man and is now living in the Irish Republic. He is still wanted in Northern Ireland to complete a sentence for terrorist offences.

23   Seamus Clarke wasn't the only team member to join the IRA. Sometime in the mid to late seventies, Maurice Gilvarry also joined up. He had been picked up by the Army during the sweeps that came with internment in 1971 and deposited in Long Kesh. At 16 he was one of the youngest internees.

24   After his release, Maurice became an active member of the Belfast IRA. Eamon Gilvarry remembers his brother seeming a great deal older when he came out of Long Kesh.

25   'In the beginning, around '68–'69, we didn't know who was in the IRA. Why did Maurice join up? To follow his mates? I never asked . . .' In fact Eamon knew nothing of his brother's secret life. And then one weekend in winter 1981, Maurice went missing. Eamon spent the weekend going around the pubs and clubs of Ardoyne trying to track him down. The following Tuesday, he switched on the lunchtime news to hear that a body had been found on the border with the Irish Republic. The man had been shot in the head and was found with his hands tied behind his back. It was Maurice. The IRA issued a statement saying he had been executed as an informer.

26   Eamon's most painful memory is of the funeral. As the coffin was being carried up through Ardoyne, he noticed a group of local Republicans standing on the corner, laughing, deliberately and ostentatiously. 'They laughed as we passed them with the coffin. I never laughed at anybody's death.'

27   And that is where the story of the boys of Holy Cross might end. Loss and grief and a certain amount of bitterness. But there is a postscript of hope. In the summer of 1998 – thirty years after the photograph was taken – there is peace in Ardoyne. The rioting and gun battles are over. The Good Friday Agreement has been signed. Children are playing on the streets outside new houses.

28   Eamon Gilvarry tells me the peace is the best chance for a generation, that he feels hope in spite of his anger. A few streets away on the Gaelic football pitch, Pat Murphy is shouting instructions to a group of youngsters, the Holy Cross team of 1998. Pat is telling them they can be winners if they make the effort. It is up to them, he says. Up to them.

Extract 2: *An Interview with Rachel O'Connor*

Rachel O'Connor is a young teacher who has returned to work in Belfast

AB: Rachel, you grew up in Belfast?

RO'C: Yes.

A: Can you tell me something about growing up there, the area you lived in, perhaps where your parents came from?

R: My mum is from the Falls Road. Dad is from north Belfast. We live in the suburbs but used to live in west Belfast – the trouble spot. I think growing up in Belfast, you don't realize how different it is from growing up elsewhere until you move away. I think it was when I started university in Birmingham – I would notice queues of traffic and think they were an army checkpoint as I was used to seeing the army on the streets and the police stopping people in their cars. It was hard to think it was just a queue of cars. Going to the shops – I would walk into say M&S and would expect someone to search my bag in case I was carrying a bomb. I remember things like hunger strikes – vague memories some of them, because it was in my childhood. St Patrick's Day – you could not wear a shamrock because it might offend someone – my Dad explained this to me. When we went on holiday – in a unionist stronghold around 12th July – bands would be parading. I wanted a Union Jack but could not have one. When I was in the upper sixth, I was working in a department store like M&S. I was working in the household section, selling blankets, duvets, etc. A woman came over and looked under a duvet and found a box. I knew it was a bomb. Yes, it really was a bomb! My immediate reaction was to run – I was frightened, but I had to tell the supervisor, who telephoned the police. The police came and confirmed it was a bomb and we had to evacuate the store. We had to make sure all the customers were out, but some people were arguing and wanted to carry on shopping. I went into another shop and they also found a bomb so they were all evacuated too. Something happened all the time; people were always looking for bombs, incendiary devices.

A: Those daily occurrences in ordinary life – queuing, having your bag searched, bombs – it sounds so difficult before the first cease-fire came. Do you remember how you felt about the cease-fire?

R: Remember it clearly. An exciting day. I was very nervous too. If there was a cease-fire it would be more difficult for them to return to the trouble – even though they could argue about it being permanent. I just wanted to think it was going to be like that for ever. People celebrating in pubs. I remember the bomb at Canary Wharf [in Docklands, London] – I was devastated. I didn't want it to go back the way it had been.

A: So, you feel life has changed considerably – do you feel the atmosphere is different at home now?

R: Yes. People there are not sure what's going to happen. People are happy. They always wanted to think things were going to be different – a feeling that you had to trust people. Although they're still nervous. They didn't know which way to vote [in the Northern Irish referendum].

A: You've been back home several times recently. Last time you went, you accepted a job teaching in an integrated school.

Rachel and some of her students at Lagan College (Rachel is second from right)

R: An integrated school takes pupils from both sides of the community – Catholic and Protestant. From 'flashpoint' areas – the children can meet each other. [there are] no other opportunities for this. It was the first such school to be set up.

A: Rachel, quite soon you'll be going off to teach a new generation of children in Northern Ireland from both communities. Have you got a message to pass on to them?

R: I think peace is the way forward. We have a lot more in common with each other [than what divides us]. Times have changed and young people want peace and to trust each other and to make the most of what we have got.

Extract 3: *Christian Aid*

This is your last chance to support our team.

At 14, Stuart and his Ethiopian friends share the same dream: to play football for their countries. Their chances of success are pretty evenly matched. But should they fail, their chances for the future are far from even.

In Ethiopia, over 50 per cent of all children never reach adulthood. And too many of those who do face a life without proper food, healthcare, or the opportunity of learning a trade. At Christian Aid, we believe children and adults should have the chance to live life, rather than simply survive it.

In countries where infant mortality is high, we help local communities to provide clean water and essential healthcare. Where levels of literacy are low, we provide education. And where there's a crisis, as in Sudan, we are there to provide essential aid.

This year's Christian Aid Week is nearly over. So if you haven't had the opportunity to give, please call 0345 000 300 or fill in the coupon now. Your support today will give thousands hope for tomorrow.

Please give now. Send the coupon or call 0345 000 300

I enclose a cheque/PO made payable to Christian Aid for: £250*☐ £200☐ £100☐ £25☐ Other £ _____

Or please debit my card. (Mastercard/Visa/Other specify) _____

Card No. ☐☐☐☐☐☐☐☐☐☐☐☐☐☐☐☐   Expiry Date _____   OW00OB/05

Signature _____   Name _____

Address _____

_____ Postcode _____

Christian ⛪ Aid
We believe in life before death

Send your donation to: Christian Aid, Freepost MR8192, Manchester M1 9AZ.
Please visit our web site www.christian-aid.org.uk
* Gift Aid   Registered Charity No 258003

Christian Aid Week. May 10–17.

Extract 4: *Speaking Out: Black Girls in Britain*

Introduction: Making our voices heard

'Girls must learn to stand up for themselves, whether they are Asian, Afro-Caribbean, English or whatever. It doesn't really matter who you are, what matters is to spend time talking about what you want to do. We've found out that we've got the same kind of ideas on many issues.'

Wealth equals power

Afia
'There shouldn't really be any poor countries in the world or any poor people, but I don't think you can stop it because the greedy countries like America just want the best for themselves. We just take what we want from these countries, like coffee for instance, and pay them very little for it. All these groups that try to help poor countries, the Red Cross for instance, all they can do is help in a crisis but they can't really stop the poverty without taking away power from the rich.'

Mumtaz
'I don't think there should be famine, not in the 1980s and 1990s. America, England and all the other rich countries should get together and do something about it. With Live Aid and Band Aid it took pop stars to do something. There was this Tory MP who said, "Well, pop stars should do something about it, it doesn't depend on us." But

they are in power, they form the government,
they have a responsibility to do something. If they
are going to say that why don't they let the pop
stars run the government?'

Nazrah
'I've never heard anyone explain that rich
countries may help maintain the poverty of these
countries by buying goods at cheap prices. They
certainly have never mentioned it in school.
They'd say it would be too controversial and there
would be quarrelling in class.'

Mumtaz
'In school you don't try to look at the whole world
and think about relationships. But we ought to
think about the whole world because famine can't
just be blamed on the people and the land and on
natural causes.'

False picture

Rasheeda
'On TV they show developing countries as poor,
they make out the people are lazy, or not exactly
lazy but not too bothered about anything, perhaps
because of the weather and the heat. They suggest
that that makes them feel like not working. I think
they should go into it more. They should look
more closely at a country's economy and those
sort of things rather than show pictures of starving
children, black starving children in particular.'

Afia

'People here, when they see the starving children, they think, "Oh, it's children starving! How terrible! We'd better be kind to them. We'd better help them!" They are not thinking about the country's relationships. They are not thinking about the way they vote. I don't think it's the responsibility of people like Bob Geldof* to make their minds up for them. I don't think he should do that because it's not his job, and he says that himself. He's just pointing out that you should look at who you're voting for. Look at the countries. Think about famine.'

Mumtaz

'I don't think that half the pop stars were really bothered about what they were raising money for. They just thought, "This will be a good image-maker for ourselves. We'll look really kind and generous and we can gain some more fans by playing live." There were some sincere ones but half of them don't know what they are there for. So they can't put it to proper use.'

Afia

'I don't think we get a very true picture. We see poor countries and people get the impression that the whole country is a desert. ITV and the BBC, they are restricted because they are trying to find pictures that will make people really look at the

---

*Bob Geldof was a pop star who raised a lot of money to help people in the third world.

news. The whole thing is so restricted. I don't know if it's true or not but it was said with the Falklands war that the Prime Minister had to approve the news in some way. If we see the news through Margaret Thatcher's* eyes we're not going to understand the vital parts of it.'

*Prime minister at the time

Extract 5: *Oxfam*

Last month
Paul helped install
3 washing machines
2 jacuzzis,
a swimming pool...

...and a well
in Mozambique

Paul gives £2 a month to Oxfam . . .

'AS A LOCAL PLUMBER my work doesn't take me far, but by giving £2 a month to Oxfam, I can help people *continents* away.

I've helped a poor village in Mozambique to install their own well, for instance. Of course, the villagers over there did the hard work.

But my £2 a month supplied the tools they used.

Now they have a well. Which means no more children dying from polluted water. Just clean, drinkable water for everyone. And all they needed was a chance to solve their own problem – to help themselves.

That's the best thing about the way Oxfam helps people.

They don't walk in with a quick-fix answer, they work <u>with</u> poor people to help them find <u>permanent</u> solutions to hunger and disease.

In their hands £2 a month goes an amazingly long way.

It might not buy much over here, but, because the people Oxfam supports put in so much hard work, every penny stretches further.

Just take a look at what YOUR £2 a month could do . . .

Your £2 a month can help people work to beat poverty.

£2 a month can help villagers dig a well.

In Mozambique, women have to walk miles to find water, and that water may be polluted with lethal germs and bacteria. £2 a month will provide tools to help their village dig a well – giving everyone in the community a supply of clean, safe water for years to come.

£2 a month can help farmers feed their families.
In Ethiopia, where the land is often parched and difficult to farm, drought can lead to widespread hunger. £2 a month will help Ethiopian farmers to plant 670 saplings, stabilizing the soil, encouraging rainfall and making the land fertile enough to grow crops again.

£2 a month can help mothers protect their children.

In India, thousands of children die every day from preventable diseases. £2 a month will train a voluntary healthworker to teach mothers how to protect their children, saving countless young lives.

Whatever you do, give £2 a month to Oxfam.

Activities

1   Explore the language used in Extract 1.
    a   Re-read the first four paragraphs. Comment on
        the use of past and present tense to report
        events, looking particularly at the tenses used in
        the direct speech and narrative in paragraph 4.
        What effect do those choices have on the
        reader?
    b   Look closely at paragraphs 6 and 22. Where do
        the changes in tense happen and why?

2   Read Extract 1.
    a   Look at paragraphs 1 to 6. Explain why Mr
        Grogan told the boys to stand where they were
        and how they felt when they were lining up for
        their photograph. What visual impression does
        this section create for the reader?
    b   Look at paragraphs 14 to 17. Why do you think
        the author began the article with a description
        of the football team before moving on to
        describe these scenes?
    c   The article ranges over recent history to the
        present day. Look at the first five paragraphs
        again. Is the atmosphere in the opening and
        closing sections the same? What effect does the
        ending have on you as reader?

3   Read Extract 2, taking particular notice of the long
    paragraph in which Rachel describes finding a bomb
    under a duvet. Write a short conversation using
    direct speech punctuation, in which you, as the
    shop assistant, politely but clearly explain to a

customer that she or he must evacuate the building. The customer is not quickly persuaded but your approach works after a short dialogue. Remember that you do not want to panic members of the public but must remain firm in your requests for their evacuation.

4   This is a simulation task which requires you to work in a small group. First, choose one of the charities advertising in Extract 3 or 5. Your group is a small company competing for a contract to manage an advertising campaign for your chosen charity. You have been asked to design a fund-raising flyer which can be inserted into Sunday newspapers. You must produce the flyer to display to representatives of the charity. You will have to show them the features of your design and answer their questions about it. Remember yours must be the best campaign, on paper and in the presentation. Pay attention to the need for eye-catching language, visual layout and key information. Desktop publishing would help you if it is available. Your class, acting as representatives of the charity, will provide the audience for your presentation.

5   Read Extracts 3 and 4. The advertiser wants us to give aid but the teenagers in Extract 4 suggest that some attempts to help do little to stop poverty. What should be done? Draw up your own list of actions which you feel would help to eliminate poverty. You could use the following headings: What individuals can do; What charities can do; What governments can do.

6   In the 1990s, state schools and examination boards in England and Wales were obliged to follow a National Curriculum which ensured that pupils were

taught similar material from the age of 5 to 16. Teachers were told what topics should be included in, for example, history and geography. In English, certain kinds of reading had to be covered. A Birmingham schoolgirl* talking in the 1980s said about the curriculum then: 'In school you don't try to look at the whole world and think about relationships. But we ought to think about the whole world because famine can't just be blamed on the people and the land and on natural causes.'

What have you learned about whole-world issues in school? Are they covered in the subject areas above, or elsewhere? Write a letter to the Minister of Education to explain how well you think these issues are covered in school and any changes you would like to see made.

---

*From *Speaking Out: Black Girls in Britain*

ALSO IN

Heinemann
New Windmills

Founding Editors: Anne and Ian Serraillier

Chinua Achebe Things Fall Apart
David Almond Skellig
Maya Angelou I Know Why the Caged Bird Sings
Margaret Atwood The Handmaid's Tale
Jane Austen Pride and Prejudice
J G Ballard Empire of the Sun
Stan Barstow Joby; A Kind of Loving
Nina Bawden Carrie's War; Devil by the Sea; Kept in the Dark; The Finding; Humbug
Lesley Beake A Cageful of Butterflies
Malorie Blackman Tell Me No Lies; Words Last Forever
Martin Booth Music on the Bamboo Radio
Ray Bradbury The Golden Apples of the Sun; The Illustrated Man
Betsy Byars The Midnight Fox; The Pinballs; The Not-Just-Anybody Family; The Eighteenth Emergency
Victor Canning The Runaways
Jane Leslie Conly Racso and the Rats of NIMH
Robert Cormier We All Fall Down
Roald Dahl Danny, The Champion of the World; The Wonderful Story of Henry Sugar; George's Marvellous Medicine; The BFG; The Witches; Boy; Going Solo; Matilda; My Year
Anita Desai The Village by the Sea
Charles Dickens A Christmas Carol; Great Expectations; Hard Times; Oliver Twist; A Charles Dickens Selection
Peter Dickinson Merlin Dreams
Berlie Doherty Granny was a Buffer Girl; Street Child
Roddy Doyle Paddy Clarke Ha Ha Ha
Anne Fine The Granny Project
Jamila Gavin The Wheel of Surya
Graham Greene The Third Man and The Fallen Idol; Brighton Rock
Thomas Hardy The Withered Arm and Other Wessex Tales
L P Hartley The Go-Between
Ernest Hemmingway The Old Man and the Sea; A Farewell to Arms
Frances Mary Hendry Chandra
Barry Hines A Kestrel For A Knave
Nigel Hinton Getting Free; Buddy; Buddy's Song; Out of the Darkness
Anne Holm I Am David

Janni Howker Badger on the Barge; The Nature of the Beast; Martin Farrell
Pete Johnson The Protectors
Jennifer Johnston Shadows on Our Skin
Geraldine Kaye Comfort Herself
Daniel Keyes Flowers for Algernon
Clive King Me and My Million
Dick King-Smith The Sheep-Pig
Elizabeth Laird Red Sky in the Morning; Kiss the Dust
D H Lawrence The Fox and The Virgin and the Gypsy; Selected Tales
George Layton The Swap
Harper Lee To Kill a Mockingbird
Julius Lester Basketball Game
C Day Lewis The Otterbury Incident
Joan Lingard Across the Barricades; The File on Fraulein Berg
Penelope Lively The Ghost of Thomas Kempe
Jack London The Call of the Wild; White Fang
Bernard MacLaverty Cal; The Best of Bernard Mac Laverty
Margaret Mahy The Haunting
Anthony Masters Wicked
James Vance Marshall Walkabout
Ian McEwan The Daydreamer; A Child in Time
Pat Moon The Spying Game
Michael Morpurgo My Friend Walter; The Wreck of the Zanzibar; The War of Jenkins' Ear; Why the Whales Came; Arthur, High King of Britain
Beverley Naidoo No Turning Back
Bill Naughton The Goalkeeper's Revenge
New Windmill A Charles Dickens Selection
New Windmill Book of Classic Short Stories
New Windmill Book of Fiction and Non-fiction: Taking Off!
New Windmill Book of Haunting Tales
New Windmill Book of Humorous Stories: Don't Make Me Laugh
New Windmill Book of Nineteenth Century Short Stories
New Windmill Book of Non-fiction: Get Real!
New Windmill Book of Non-fiction: Real Lives, Real Times
New Windmill Book of Scottish Short Stories
New Windmill Book of Short Stories: Fast and Curious
New Windmill Book of Short Stories: Tales with a Twist

How many have you read?